LIFE, FAITH AND PRAYER

A. GRAHAM IKIN
M.A., M.Sc.

Life, Faith and Prayer

WITH AN INTRODUCTORY
NOTE BY

LESLIE D. WEATHERHEAD
M. A., PH. D., D. D.

NEW YORK
OXFORD UNIVERSITY PRESS
1954

INTRODUCTORY NOTE

by Leslie D. Weatherhead

ALL who, like myself, have taken a deep interest in the co-operation of clergy and doctors, have noted, with admiration, the fine work done by Miss A. Graham Ikin in this field. The late Archbishop Temple had this matter very much on his mind and created what was called 'The Archbishop of York's Committee of Doctors and Clergy.' Of this Committee Miss Ikin acted as Secretary and itinerant lecturer, and out of this Committee was born the Churches' Council of Healing. Miss Ikin's books and work have illustrated her insight into the value both of psychology and religion as integrating factors of personality, and this present book can only add to her reputation. Her religion has never been the narrow, sectarian type, nor has her psychology been imprisoned in the thought-forms of any one particular school. Many things are said in the enclosed book which will help the minister, teacher, doctor and parent, and indeed any reader concerned with the inner well-being of other people and the health of his own soul.

PREFACE

Each age and generation has to face fundamental problems for itself, seeing them in the perspective of its own type of experience and cultural background. Always there is some tension between those who seek to conserve the form of the past at the expense of the growing spirit which needs to clothe itself afresh to be appropriate to the present, and those who tend to disown the past, instead of discerning the creative elements within it which could lead on to a *continuity of development* in which all that is of permanent value from the past is conserved while the changing needs of a different age are also met.

We have mastered *external* nature sufficiently to be able to maintain life in huge cities, and have found ourselves faced with fresh problems, both individually and corporately as a result. We have also become more conscious of ourselves and of our relationships with each other, which has brought a psychological attitude to bear upon many problems which had previously been thought to be purely external and which are now seen to be projected onto events from within our own nature. Even in Physics the observer and the observed are realised to form a unity, and observation involves *both* subjective and objective elements.

This applies even more in the social, psychological and religious spheres. What we *are* conditions what we are able to perceive. On some levels this distinction is more important than others. A doctor's training, for example, leads him to notice significance in much that escapes the untrained mind, and the same is true in all professions and skills. The mind of each is trained as a selective filter that allows what is irrelevant to it to slip through. The trouble comes when the various specialists about the section of experience they have selected as their particular province think that what has gone through *their* particular filter unnoticed does not exist.

7

For practical skill each *has* to specialise, but unless each specialist is aware of the bias his point of view inevitably brings in and checks up his findings against a wider background, the one-sidedness will in the long run effect even his specialised practice adversely more than he is likely to realise. He is then likely to blame pupil, patient or client, as the case may be, for the failure that may rest with himself.

One of the major conflicts occurs between those who believe in a Creative Mind, responsible for and expressing itself through nature, the world in which we live and in and through mankind, i.e. a God who genuinely *creates*, and those who think in terms of a scientific determinism which leaves no room for creative activity, either human or Divine.

The problem is a very real one for those trained in a scientific discipline through which *predictable* sequences seem to confirm a deterministic and orderly background of events, and who cannot reconcile this with some of the vagaries of religious interpretations and experience which seem to imply an arbitrary 'Will' liable to upset all preconceived calculations. Whereas those who have first-hand experience in which they seem to discover the influence of an over-ruling Providence which they *can increasingly trust*, which is therefore no longer conceived as 'arbitrary', sometimes think the scientists' respect for the order of nature and patient research into the ways in which things behave, the specific 'go-togetherness' of events, as unnecessary and even an impious attempt to usurp God's prerogative and to gain control from a humanistic standpoint.

In this book it is hoped to at least adumbrate a synthesis on a higher level which will make it possible for both scientific and religious thinkers to respect and allow for the reality of *both* responses of the human mind to life and experience.

The first chapter sets the stage for this by emphasising the need for both *scientific thinking and religious experience*,

not only for the living of a good life, but for the mainten-
ance of human life with its complicated social structures
at all.

In 'Adam and Eve' the continuity of physical and spiritual
aspects of sex on the human level is stressed, with its prehuman history and its personal relationships and cultural
influence within a social and religious framework or environment. Here is a linking element *par excellence* with the creativity and determinism united in the *uniqueness* of every genuine
expression of the love of man and woman, which nevertheless
depends for its fulfilment on the co-ordination and integration of innumerable processes which are common to all
mankind.

In 'Finding the Self in Society', a synthesis in a third,
spiritually mature, development of self-consciousness, which
transcends the first two stages in infancy and adolescence
during middle age, though it involves changes well symbolised
as 're-birth', is shown to be a fulfilment and not a destruction
of the earlier levels of development. In this, instead of an
artificial splitting of the world into natural and supernatural
realms in *opposition* to each other, the spiritual and the physical
are seen to be mutually dependent in a Universe in which
Incarnation is a Reality. Spirit, as the late Dr. William Temple
stressed, exists by means of matter, and matter exists *for* the
expression of spirit in a sacramental universe.

In 'Youth and Middle Age' this idea is carried further
through the recognition of three phases or stages in religious
development with emphasis on God the Father in the first,
on the Incarnate Christ in the second, and on the indwelling
of the Holy Spirit in the third.

In 'Problems of Maturity' the climacteric is shown to
involve not only a physical change, an alteration of glandular
balance, with its physical and psychological effects, but to
offer a spiritual opportunity to press forward to the higher
reaches of spiritual experience and activities as physical

capacity diminishes, which can deepen culture and make for an inspiring old age.

In 'Fallen Angel or Risen Ape?' man's place in the Cosmos is considered and the *grounds* giving rise to each side of the antithesis are allowed for, thus transcending both in a way that may enable protagonists of either view to accept a synthesis of an element of truth from their own side that they cannot honestly explain away, with that which from the other point of view seems more superficially to contradict it.

'Psychology and Prayer' is written for those who believe in God and in various ways pray to Him. It indicates an interpenetration of the human and the Divine such that real prayer is a *response* to the impact of the Mind of God on His human creatures, which leads to an increasing awareness of the presence of God.

'Further Notes on Prayer' indicate some practical problems that arise through the *reliability* of God and His equal concern for the welfare of *all*, which may help us to align ourselves more truly with His purposes, and so find the fulfilment of our *real* needs, which are His concern as well as ours.

It is hoped that the cumulative effect of this blending of scientific thinking and religious experience on so many levels may evoke flashes of insight into the eternal background to all our experience, which is timelessly operative *within* the temporal sequence.

My thanks are due to the Editor of the *Guardian* for kind permission to reproduce 'Psychology and Prayer', which first appeared as a series of articles in it, and also to the Editor of the *London and Holborn Review*, in which 'Scientific Thinking and Religious Experience' was published.

CONTENTS

LIFE, FAITH AND PRAYER

CHAPTER I

Scientific Thinking and Religious Experience

SOME time ago I was travelling through a long tunnel when a waiter approached me, bowed deferentially and said 'Will you have plain cake or currant cake, Madam?' I thought of Aladdin's lamp and that not all the wealth of Eastern imagination could have conjured up anything more wonderful than being offered the choice of plain cake or currant cake in a small room, beautifully uphostered, well warmed and lighted, travelling at a great speed right under a mountain. Yet this had become such a commonplace of every-day activity that it was taken for granted.

The possibility of such a marvellous happening was the result of much co-operation, involving the pooling of know-ledge in many interrelated subjects, as well as its practical application by engineers and workmen, as well as railway officials, not to mention confectioners and salesmen.

The whole of our everyday life is permeated with the products of scientific thinking. If all scientific thinking was suddenly removed, we should not only be unable to live the *good* life, but we should be unable to live any life at all. I read a novel some time ago in which the collapse of civilisa-tion was pictured, when some rapid intra-atomic dissolution of metals took place, and all the iron, steel or other metal machinery broke down. In a few weeks only a few hordes of savages, reduced to cannibalism to live at all, were left of our modern world, except for a few scientists who, like Noah of old, had seen what was coming and prepared a modern ark, stored with food enough to last twelve months; while they strove to use their scientific thinking to produce a substitute metal that would not rot, in the hope of saving a fraction of mankind to carry life forward. Since then the discovery of atomic bombs has brought the possibility of this 'phantasy' into the realm of sober fact.

This brought home very forcibly how dependent we now are upon this comparatively recently developed capacity of man to think scientifically. Wherein does it differ from another, much older capacity, which we call religious experience? And what part does religious experience play in a world so dependent upon scientific thinking? Is it to be outgrown as childish and infantile, to be transcended by scientific thinking? Some scientists would have us think so. But one thing is sure—that scientific thinking makes it impossible to rest content with a superstitious and infantile religion. Religious experience, which so far as we know is as early as man himself, has developed through many strange and often ugly and repelling forms. It bears the marks of its history within it, and the science that condemns its superstitions and childishness should challenge us to grow up religiously as well as scientifically.

The fact that the products of scientific thinking (which are essential to our existence under modern conditions) can be used for the common good, or turned against one section of the community by another in war, civil or international, seems to indicate also that something more than scientific thinking is necessary if we are to continue to live at all. May it not be that it is the weakness, superstition and childishness of our religion that makes civil wars possible and rouses anxiety lest world war should again become inevitable? May the hope of averting disaster depend upon our ability to purge our religion of its childishness and to grow towards the maturity of religious response to Reality expressed in the life of Christ?

If so, if the challenge is to grow up religiously as well as scientifically, in order to avoid the actual developments of science in the hands of men and women, destroying through modern warfare the civilisation that has been produced by it, can we use scientific thinking to clarify and purify our religious experience?

In the succeeding chapters I hope to show that we can, and that the consideration of all the religious problems involved in the various subjects is greatly illumined by insight gained by psychological workers, not all of whom would call themselves religious. Psychotherapy, which means the *healing of the mind*, is bringing many of the Gospel miracles within the realm of present experience. The application of some of the psychological principles (discovered through the practical therapeutic work in curing patients) within the sphere of the mental health of the community and the effect of this on both physique and culture, the attitude towards crime, delinquency and other forms of misconduct, together with insight into aids and hindrances in the realm of prayer, are a rich indication of the value of scientific thinking in deepening our religious experience and enabling it to bring forth fruit in the everyday world in which we live.

Before going to this application in detail, however, it is necessary to go back to a question raised near the beginning, namely, what is the difference between scientific thinking and religious experience? And how can each play its part in the communal life of mankind?

But there is one difficulty which must first be considered. If, as some scientists have held, science leaves no room for the reality of God, then all religious experience, and any attempt to interpret history in the light of the unfolding of a Divine purpose, is illusory. Religious experience on this view is a flight from reality and not a closer approximation to it. So let us first see what evidence we can find, *apart from religious experience itself*, which makes another interpretation possible and which will allow for the reality of God and therefore for conceptions and *mis*conceptions of this Reality.

The question at some stage in the life of every genuine scientific thinker becomes a very real one; not just a matter of academic interest, but a life-and-death struggle within himself. Has the pursuit of Truth, which has illumined so much of his way and led him to realise its ultimate and absolute value, led him to where he must discard his religion? A genuine agnosticism, as Professor Malinowski pointed out, is a tragic and shattering state of mind. And those who have not had to face the issue have no right to find fault with those who have been unable to find a way of reconciling their scientific and religious activity.

What follows now was written at a time when I was struggling with the problem myself, and so, because it was written in response to the challenge of life and not merely from an intellectual or academic point of view, it may be helpful to others.

'The inability to distinguish between the product of our imagination and reality, which marks the infancy of the individual and of the race, is at the root of many of our troubles; yet without the right use of imagination our mental and moral development is atrophied and contact with reality is lost.

'The great question is: Is the universe with God at its heart the real world? Does Reality honour our cheques on God, so to speak, or is it only the phantasy construction of the human mind, and the real world therefore one in which all response to the apparent call of God is illusory?

'The question is torturing many people today who have dabbled in modern psychology without going deep enough into it to get through the chaos and confusion of our unconscious minds to the fundamental reality in which they are grounded.

'With regard to whether a godless universe is the real one or the phantastic one, on facing it out we find that if the godless universe were real, so much is falsified that in the end reason itself is suspect and there is no court of appeal left. As I look round my room now I see signs of real co-ordination and co-operation instanced by my gas fire, my electric light, some Japanese prints which I love for their beauty, which had involved colour printing in Japan and shipping and transport to England. So that it is evident that there is some intelligence available; not to speak of my own in attempting to tackle the problem!

'The godless universe, which carried to its logical conclusion denies the reality of the intelligence by which it has been postulated, would therefore seem to be the phantastic one, since reality is not as insane and incoherent as all that.

'The result of intelligent, purposive and co-operative activity on the part of almost the whole world, actually expressed in my room, which includes not only Japanese workmanship, but towels from Cyprus, prints from Egypt and India, chocolate from the cocoa plantations, as well as home products such as gas and electricity, and many others in furniture, hangings and carpets, seems to imply that *Reality responds to the intelligence and goodwill of men* (the goodwill is instanced by the co-operation necessary for such a collection of international products of pooled intelligence), that is to say, *Reason seems to be at the heart of Reality, which I suppose is what we mean by God.*

'Our sanity too seems to depend upon the reality of God. In pushing logically to its limits the godless universe, we can find no means of knowing whether we really exist or not. God, the world and ourselves seem either all to come to pieces together, with no cohesion or reality, an appalling phantasmagoria of futility: or with the return of reason, our real selves find themselves in a real world, depending upon the reality of God, *in the sense of orderly purposive controlling intelligence.*

'The words of the late King George V's broadcast at Christmas 1933 come into my mind as relevant here. "Unshakeable sanity, invincible patience and tireless goodwill" were, he said, "the foundation for seeing us through the difficulties ahead." And in that, wherever it might appear, we find the reality of God. It is a short step then to seeing *that* embodied in Christ on Calvary. For there was a sanity that no outward circumstance broke, a patience that saw it through, and a tireless goodwill that forgave His crucifiers, pardoned the penitent thief and provided for His mother. These things were real, whatever the result, whether Calvary was the end or no. And this brings the realisation that the reality of Jesus of Nazareth guarantees the reality of human personality. If he is real, we can never be pantheistically absorbed in God. The reason, patience and goodwill embodied or incarnate in Him, were incarnate in a real historical person. It was not just universal mind, but the mind of Jesus. Hence in some odd way He guarantees God and Man, or both dissolve into phantasy; which seems to make Christ central to our world in some unique way.'

We have faced the possibility of religious experience being illusory and found some grounds for believing the universe is not only fundamentally rational but also good. The response to co-operation throughout the world to bring together the products of pooled human intelligence within my room was used to illustrate this. The destructive effects of ill-will in modern warfare illustrates the same point. We co-operate up to a point in killing each other: and vanquished and victor alike suffer. If we could co-operate whole-heartedly throughout the world, *without fear of each other*, we could see to it that no one starved; and if we combined to fight disease, then disease too could be eliminated. It is the ability to love our neighbour as ourselves that we lack, though this is very largely the result of our unwillingness to face the 'evil', irrational or shadow side of ourselves, which we then project onto our neighbour and fight as external, instead of coming to grips with our own inner problems.

Perhaps we can now get clear what is the difference between scientific thinking and religious experience.

Suppose for a moment we had achieved the miracle of universal goodwill. Suppose throughout the world all men everywhere desired the goodwill of their fellows and were prepared to work and suffer to achieve it, as the best men and women are now. Would that desire, in harmony with the mind of God, who has no favourites, be sufficient to clothe and educate the human race? Would a world that genuinely put personal values highest, a world on a religious basis, be able to dispense with 'scientific thinking' in its attempt to build the Kingdom of God on earth?

The earlier part of this chapter indicates that the answer to this will be 'No'. We cannot simply pray 'let there be light' in the dark hours, where light may make all the difference in a difficult childbirth, for example. But as a result of many men humbly striving to discover how things actually work in God's universe, we can by the turn of a switch flood a room with light.

So throughout life under material conditions we need the kind of knowledge that comes from scientific thinking, which seeks to discover how things behave, and which learns to control the forces or energies we find in nature by understanding. But the attempt to be exact in scientific thinking introduces a definite limitation. If we know everything about any one thing, we should also know something about everything else, as Tennyson pointed out with his ' flower in a crannied wall'. Since we cannot start by this, we take certain aspects of any object or phenomenon we wish to understand *and for the time being ignore* other aspects. The different natural sciences are the products of extensive knowledge of particular aspects of the universe. These aspects are never found separately in reality, but each of them is found *concurrently* throughout a whole section of experience. Chemistry and physics, for example, both deal with the material universe, though with different aspects of it. The trouble comes when scientists forget they have taken great trouble to isolate some particular aspect in order to investigate its nature. Because they can explain phenomena within the competence of their abstraction without life, consciousness or God, if they then say that life, consciousness and God have no real existence they go beyond their chosen subject matter.

Consciousness in particular, as well as life and God, is mentioned here, because one school of modern psychology, that of the Behaviourists, attempts to eliminate consciousness too, making the whole of man's complicated behaviour a product of what is technically called 'conditioned reflexes'. We can learn something even from these about the way we do actually learn by experience. But if the whole of man's evolution depended upon this mechanical conditioning, the Behaviourists would logically still have to postulate a Supreme manager of the conditions to bring about the growth and progress there has been through response to the environment, instead of a dead level of mechanical existence. The Behaviourist seems to be dealing with the mind of man on a primitive level, whereon he does act largely mechanically in response to environment, and God's guidance is chiefly external. But they do not seem to realise the significance of a queer immature creature such as man actually trying to find why he behaves as he does and then trying to *alter* that behaviour. Intelligence cannot ultimately be explained in mechanical terms. There is a difference between a billiard ball, rolling where it is pushed, and a man standing in the track, seeing a train coming along a single line to the junction of a double one and being able to tell from the way the switch is turned along which line the train will come, and either standing still or getting out of the way accordingly.

To get back to our point that scientific thinking gives us definite and precise information about certain aspects of experience, but because of its deliberate concentration on these aspects is not able to give us full information about experience. For some purposes scientific knowledge is necessary and reliable, because those aspects which fall outside its range are relatively negligible. The beauty of a picture, for example, is negligible when considering how large a space to reserve for it in a luggage van. Its weight and size are essential. But for the artist, the beauty is primary, weight and size secondary.

This brings us to another way of responding to reality, another aspect of reality. The beauty of an opal is quite as real as its hardness and size; but in complete darkness, with no light to be refracted through it, though its hardness and size are unchanged, the beauty has gone. It does not reside only in itself, but in *itself in a suitable environment*, in this case light. It is not necessary for our purpose here to go into the vexed problem as to whether beauty is in the eye of the beholder, or in the illuminated opal, or the relation between them. It is sufficient to indicate that some elements in the beauty of the opal depend on its capacity for differential refraction of light and that that beauty can only be perceived when suitably illumined; though any beauty of form will still be apprehensible to touch, since shape, size and hardness remain in the absence of light.

Through an appreciation of beauty in nature the artist feels he too illumines an aspect of experience, as much a part of reality as that measured by the scientist. In various forms, poetry or prose, sculpture or painting, he seeks to portray something of the nature of reality as *he* sees it.

Does religious experience reveal yet another aspect? Can we, while utilising all that art and science can tell us, get even deeper into reality in religious experience?

We must take into account as a fundamental fact that human nature will not be satisfied without the expression of emotion and action based on some measure of contact with the unseen ground of our existence.

We might use this to illustrate the difference in the quality of life which responds to God consciously, and reveals by the fruits of that response other human qualities not revealed in the experience of the non-religious man. The latter cuts himself off from the stimulus of the Divine environment, in so far as it depends upon his conscious attitude and limits himself to such human qualities as depend upon his *unconscious* dependence, apart from which he would not exist at all.

Otto stresses a unique element in our experience, continuous from grisly demonic horror in the presence of the *felt* unseen to awe in the Presence of the Unspeakably Holy, as running throughout our religious experience. Though his emphasis on the supra-rational and wholly other (like all over-simplifications of so complex an experience as the religion of man) tends to ignore other elements equally essential to any mature religion, Otto has done us a great service in bringing to the fore this corrective to our modern tendency to deify our rationality at the expense of the integrity of human personality, which includes affective elements, impervious to reason, yet with a relevance essential to the harmonious development of the individual, as well as to healthy communal life. *Mysterium tremendum, mysterium fascinans*, expresses a deep religious attitude.

Jung also stresses the importance of harmony between these deep-seated affective tendencies and our conscious aims and ideals. Their divergence on the basis of a narrow intellectualism, which represses the life of feeling as childish, is responsible for many nervous troubles, and for Jung, the problem of their cure is ultimately a religious one.

Whitehead points out that experience includes 'brute alogical fact'. Life is always wider than logic. Two and two only equals four in the realm of mathematical abstraction. The moment actuality is involved an irreducible surd is introduced, and unless insight can take this logically (but not necessarily intuitively) irrational element into account, prediction is always contradicted by experience.

It may be logically absurd to suggest that feeling is the

warp that produces the curvature of space-time responsible for material existence [1]: but it is less absurd than suggesting that the fundamental reality on which this phenomenal world is based, or of which it is the expression, riddled as it is with distortions of logical procedure and mathematical inconsistencies, is a passionless mathematician. Feeling must be as integral a part of fundamental or ultimate reality as of the universe in which feeling, creative or destructive, in terms of love cr hate, is the great dynamic. God as Father is a more adequate symbol for this than God as a mathematician: though the relation of this Eternal ultimate reality to all that exists involves mathematical elements throughout. Love may not be exhaustively expressed by an equation, but it cannot exist apart from a nexus of interrelations which *can* be expressed in mathematical symbols. We falsify reality by ignoring the mathematical and therefore inevitable element in experience as much as by ignoring the qualitative apprehension of that fundamental order which is beauty, goodness or love. Reality is neither quantitative nor qualitative in isolation: but *both are aspects of a universal continuum, within which all that has been, is, or can be, is vitally interrelated.*

In *The Structure of Religious Experience*, Professor Macmurray works out very clearly the fundamental nature of the facts of experience on which religion is based. He points out that in science utility dominates; we seek to control and use the forces of nature by insight and understanding, whereas in art intrinsic values matter most. We appreciate, contemplate and enjoy things for themselves. But these two attitudes towards experience, both selecting from the world of everyday experience, are transcended in a third attitude which combines both, in which personal relations dominate or are central. This sphere, according to Professor Macmurray, is the sphere of religion.

---

[1] This is not meant to be taken as a 'scientific' explanation, it is only an illustration to emphasise the absurdity of materialism.

When we organise our whole life so that personal relations are genuinely central, so that, in fact, we love our neighbour as ourselves and use our scientific thinking for the common good and dedicate our sense of beauty to bring it within the reach of all, we are living in touch with reality on the level of religion.

It is true, as Macmurray says, that science, art and religion alike claim the whole universe as their field: but it is as if out of this whole experience there are three centres of interest round which science, art and religion develop respectively. But, as he says, *religion is more comprehensive because it includes ourselves and our interrelations with each other, which transcend and transform the natural world considered independently of personal purposes.*

Because personal relations, while actually inescapable, are yet the most difficult to adjust adequately, religion often falls below its high estate and concentrates on tradition or ceremonial, becoming meticulous to fulfil the law, while leaving genuine human needs unsatisfied. Christ was crucified because He put human needs before tradition, because He healed on the Sabbath, for example; because He showed that love for God which was not expressed in the service of our fellow men, was not love of the real God He called Father; because He could take little children and say 'of such is the kingdom of Heaven' and could tell an elder of the Church of His day, a specialist in religion in the most religious nation, that he must be born again before he could even see the Kingdom of God; because He could say the publicans and harlots would go into the kingdom of Heaven before the self-righteous superior Pharisee; because He spoke in terms of our common humanity, that made the needs of each one of us, however lowly, the concern of Almighty God, irrespective of rank or creed (witness the parable of the Good Samaritan); because He lived and worked within the common round of human toil, and instead of claiming exemption as leader, washed the feet of His disciples, which each was too proud to do for the other. In all this He showed that in meeting real human needs, in doing 'the job that is under our nose, with the tools that come to our hand', we find ourselves in fellowship with Christ, who was always moved to compassion by the sufferings of others; and find through this we are fellow workers with God, within the sphere of true religion.

Professor Macmurray points out the combination of utilitarian and intrinsic valuation in religion. He says:

'Religion has always been associated with the need that men have felt for help and assistance, and part of the religious attitude has always looked upon religion as a practical means of achieving its end. But it is equally certain that religion has always looked upon its activities as important in themselves, imbued with an intrinsic value of their own. Primitive religious ceremonial is both an expression of the sense of beauty and a means of securing the welfare of the tribe. The Lord who is to be worshipped in the beauty of holiness is also a very present help in time of trouble. Christianity has always insisted on the absolute intrinsic value of the individual. But it has also equally insisted that his value lies in doing the will of God and making himself the instrument of a divine purpose.' [1]

The field of religious experience is the sphere of personal relations. Where these are the centre of valuation, we ask, not how much money will this produce, but what quality of manhood will it develop, what range of fellowship will it make possible? We then inevitably come into contact with God on the level of personality and cannot rest content with a God who is less than personal. We may bow defiantly before a god of Force: we can worship a God who loves. And in proportion as our worship is sincere, we combine the paradoxes we mentioned previously. For an apprehension of God, worshipped spontaneously, as the Supreme Value brings with

[1] J. Macmurray, *The Structure of Religious Experience*, p. 34.

it a measure of communion which *is* the help in time of trouble and involves a realisation of fellowship which fulfills the will of God for men.

The task of religion, as Professor Macmurray put it, is the realisation of fellowship. *The religious activity of the self is its effort to enter into Communion with the Other.*

Whitehead, in his Lowell lectures, said, 'Religion is what the individual does with his solitariness.'[1] I would prefer to say religion is what we make of our experience in common. The measure of the maturity of our religion is not the number of hours we can spend on our knees, but the width and depth of the range of our understanding and sympathy with men and women of different cultures, capacities and training. The range of our friendships, which can cut through differences of class prejudice and behaviour and rejoice in our common humanity with those of different races and creeds, is the test in *life* of the reality of our religion. But the achieving of a wide community of interest is no easy thing. It can only be achieved through a fuller realisation of the form of our own religion, the sharing more deeply in the cultural and national level of life; not by ignoring differences, not by levelling down can true fellowship come, but by a deepening of our own personal life in relation to the form and structure of the society in which we live until its universal aspect *permeates* its particular mode of expression. From the universal and eternal fellowship with the God who is Father of all we can then enter into fellowship with others whose ways of approach have been so different that any attempt at communion on a lower level would inevitably clash. Once again the insight of Christ is seen to be supreme. It is necessary to 'love God with all our hearts, minds and strength' before we *can* 'love our neighbour as ourself'. It is within this sphere of personal relationships that religion moves; and where it is central, with the Supreme Personality of God as the ground of our common

[1] Prof. Whitehead, *Religion in the Making*, p. 6.

relationships with others, we may hope to use our scientific thinking to fulfil the Gospel command to preach the Gospel and heal the sick more effectively than has yet been possible.

Scientific thinking, though it abstracts certain aspects of experience, is tested throughout by its correspondence with experience. When once it ceases to bring its abstractions and hypotheses to the test of experiment and experience, it ceases to be scientific thinking and becomes speculative.

So with religious experience. *Unless it illumines and is effective within the sphere of personal life and history, individual and racial, it fails to be religious.* Any speculations as to future life in another world that are not based upon genuine insight into experience and actuality in *this* life are doomed to an illusory existence within the mind of the dreamer who postulated them, because he had neither the courage nor the sincerity to find God within the everyday life of the world in which we are so placed that we may learn to know and love God as He is, and not as our childish phantasies may desire Him to be.

It is true that our ideas of God are inadequate and fall short of the Reality. Our ideas may be only symbolical, but the symbols refer to that which is real and the very ground from which our symbolism springs.[1]

Hence such symbols may be dynamic, bridging the gulf between the finite and the infinite, so that they are not wholly and antithetically separated, but fall within a unitary comprehension; such dynamic symbolism, for example, as that of the Kingdom of God allows for the dependence of created being and the supremacy of God in perfect harmony. Such symbolism Plato considered to be essential to express the

---

[1] Cf. 'But the fact that the conception (i.e. of God) does work in human experience, that it does enable men to conform to the requirements of the world in which they are placed and to achieve fuller life, is evidence for the contention that the conception is not an illusion, but that however inadequate it may be it is at least symbolical of ultimate Reality.' Wright's *Philosophy of Religion*, p. 357.

nature of ultimate realities, beyond the grasp of the discursive intellect. For him effective symbolism, while it could not express exhaustively the nature of reality involved, was essentially related to it and thus was a medium for revelation.

If Plato had lived after Christ and carried this idea further, in the light of personality, he would have found in the Incarnation the completion of the process of symbolism, through which the Divine Mind revealed itself at last as perfectly personal. The religious response to Reality would then find its fulfilment in communion with the Christ, who had thus embodied the symbol in life, and not merely in thought, thus united men with the God to whom they owed their origin.

CHAPTER II

Adam and Eve

THE allegory of Adam and Eve illustrates both a likeness and a difference in the emotional attitudes of men and women; covered with shame, caught in something felt to be wrong, neither was prepared to accept the blame, to accept the responsibility for their own actions. Adam blamed Eve, Eve blamed the serpent; but as Dr. Hadfield once said, 'God was not deceived and He drove *them* out of the garden.'

The likeness is expressed by a common desire to repudiate responsibility. But Adam blames his partner in the act, apart from whom he could have had no pleasure, and shows a meanness that is often historically repeated. Eve with a deeper intuition blames an element symbolised by the serpent, from which an unclean element had come in to spoil their relationship. But in either case *it was their own response* that each repudiated that was important.

Sex is a factor in the course of evolution long before human beings appear on the scene, and its prehuman history colours its expression on our own level. The serpent in many mythologies symbolises this elemental force or form of sex, prehuman, not yet lifted to the plane of human behaviour and emotion. And where this primitive, prehuman level creeps in, our genuine humanity feels ashamed. We fall below the possibilities of our real nature; and our shame is an expression of our potentialities for a higher manifestation of the sexual principle than is possible on the subhuman level.

In order, however, to achieve the fullest emotional and personal development possible to us, we have to accept and not repudiate the presence in us of this non-moral, elemental driving-force. If it can drag us to the depths, it can also raise us to the heights. It can be destructive or creative of moral values, according to our attitude to it. As Mr. Metman has finely said, 'frenzy and reverence' must unite.

Sex is a great creative impulse, which can both torture us and bless us. Unfortunately, partly through St. Paul's attitude to sex and still more from that of St. Augustine, it has been difficult to get a true acceptance of sex as a means through which the eternal purpose of creation is carried forward. The possibility, so frequently actual, of an unclean or alien element associated with sexual activity, led to a condemnation of sex itself as a lower or sinful thing. Since our nature is sexual and life can only be carried on through bisexual activity, there is an inevitable conflict between the physical expression of sex as an animal function and the psychical aspect expressed as a spiritual harmony if these are kept distinct. We cannot avail ourselves of the creative power of sex if we are ashamed of the primitive. Sex will not be so divided. It is a pervasive factor affecting all life, linking body and mind indissolubly.

In our attempt to separate the physical and psychical aspects of it we sterilise it and lose our birthright as men and women. One wonders what would have been the result if Adam and Eve had been mature enough to accept responsibility for their action—could evolution have continued in the Garden of Eden? The suggestion may give us a hint as to the direction towards Paradise Regained:

The difficulties of marriage and courtship are an expression of the value of a truly personal relationship in which the differences between the sexes find their fulfilment in mutual harmony. If sex were only an affair of the body we should have no problems about divorce. It is the psychological adjustment to sex differences that is important.

We have to adapt both to our own sexual needs as well as to the difference in attitude engendered by the biological difference of function.

The division of function between men and women biologically is of great importance here. The psychological attitude of a woman who has to be able to carry an unborn child for many months inevitably differs from that of the man, who, if promiscuous and unscrupulous, may not even know when he has begotten a child. The difference goes far back. The quicker moving, active spermatozoa and the heavier, slower ovum which waits to be fertilised, are the forerunners of the right of the man to woo and the woman to be wooed. The reaction against this, as implying inferiority on the part of the woman, is a reaction which is not likely to be permanent. In the main it expresses a revolt against the idea of a woman as merely an instrument for sexual pleasure, as wife, mistress or prostitute, and not as a *human* partner with a personality capable of satisfying man as a developed personality and not merely a sexual animal. Once it is recognised that the emotional life of women, though it may differ in some respects from that of men, is of equal cultural importance with that of man, the feeling of inferiority implied in being wooed instead of wooing will disappear.

But to achieve this men will also have to grow more mature in their attitude to women. We are more sex-conscious to-day probably than ever before. We are on the verge of a new phase in human history and are showing signs of a stormy adolescence. Sex before, good or bad, was taken for granted as a physical phenomena of nature. To-day it is being recognised as a *pervasive influence affecting the whole of our lives.* It will require finer personalities to achieve harmony in sex relationship within this wider universe, wherein the man-woman relationship is no longer one of superiority or inferiority, but is based upon a recognition of the equality of importance of their *difference in function.*

The man who learns through his wife to adjust to an eternal feminine element in himself, is a more complete, more highly developed human being than the man who repudiated the feminine aspects of his personality and consequently looked down upon the woman whom he yet used to bolster up his self esteem and satisfy his pleasure. The woman who likewise learns to adapt to a masculine element in herself becomes more, not less, womanly, since this element, too, is a fundamental capacity making for harmony with men. Inferiority and superiority no longer come in in such a relationship; and a major cause of friction and misunderstanding is removed.

Moreover, such a development, bringing into the fullest harmony complementary aspects of life, is also creative on the cultural level. The social and spiritual influence of such mature personalities is far reaching and many less mature people can find in them a spiritual father or mother, through relation to whom their infantile reactions to their own parents, which they had never adjusted adequately, can be re-adjusted. Sexual behaviour has to be relevant to the cultural and religious level of the community involving legal, economic and social obligations, and not merely the instinctive satisfaction of the sex impulse, if 'marriage' is to be successful.

It is important to realise that full sexual development on the human level includes adaptation, not only to the partner physiologically and psychologically, but also adaptation to one's sex impulses, and to the social environment within which union is to be expressed, as well as to the eternal or cosmic element in all truly human experience.

In proportion to the degree of development of the human beings concerned, so the emphasis changes from physiological to psychological, and from psychological to spiritual. But all these elements are involved throughout. Even in primitive tribes, sexual relations, whatever their social form, seem to be subject to certain 'taboos' connected with religion. However primitive the correlation, fertility and religion have been closely associated in the human mind—barrenness has often been conceived as a curse of punishment from God. It is therefore no new thing to realise that sexual satisfaction must be in harmony with religious conviction if psychological health is to be achieved. Our modern problem seems to be how to eliminate the Puritan attitude towards sex, allowing for its fullest development, without leading to licence or exploitation.

Greater freedom of discussion between men and women today is healthier than the Victorian attitude with its double standard of morality and the division of women into two classes, respectable and prostitutes. The complete separation of a man's attitude towards his family and responsibilities as a parent, and the satisfaction of physical desires, was very harmful.

We are finding today that the development of character able to stand up to the general stress of life without breaking down depends upon having an ideal purpose great enough to harmonise and utilise all our instinctive energies.

If we satisfy our impulses in ways that do not satisfy our neighbours we shall not long remain happy ourselves, since the need for social approval is very deep-seated. An instance of this is the fact that 'solitary confinement' is considered one of the most severe forms of punishment.

Is monogamy biologically and spiritually a sound ideal? Can trial marriages and companionate marriages or other extra-marital relationships play a helpful part in developing our many-sided personalities? Some of the younger generation are experimenting in this way. Some of them at least feel that the older traditional attitude has produced so many unhappy marriages that a 'trial trip' is genuinely better than committing themselves for life with mutual reaction to physical intimacy unknown.

It is possible to sympathise with this desire to make a real success of marriage, in spite of realising that this method is not likely to be successful for various reasons.

In the first place, 'trial marriages' do not reproduce the actual conditions of marriage, and are not a fair test. The psychological attitude of both partners is very different from that in a marriage *socially accepted* and *intended to be permanent*. Secondly, where the 'trial' fails, it is harder on the girl than on the man. There is a closer connection between the sexual and the maternal aspects of life in a woman than between the sexual and paternal in a man. The breakdown of a relationship which should lead on to motherhood is more distressing and serious than for a man. While, in addition, the girl is also at a greater disadvantage than the man, when it comes to 'trying again'. Men are still inconsistent in preferring a wife who has not had previous sex experience, in spite of condoning their own 'wild oats'. To fail in a 'trial marriage' may end in the woman drifting into casual sex-relationships as the hope of a satisfactory marriage recedes. Men who indulge in casual relations have not the same qualms about previous experience on the part of their partner as when contemplating marriage.

It will be seen here that I have not referred to either religious or social disapproval, but simply to differences in the nature of men and women which seem to render 'trial marriages' unsatisfactory.

We are all questioning traditional authority in various ways, and if we can find some grounds for aiming at true monogamy as the ideal towards which the relationship of the two sexes is leading, we may be able to rehabilitate the 'family' as a unit and so help to provide the most essential background for children. So many nervous disorders spring from domestic disharmonies in childhood, and it is important to realise that every happy and successful marriage is helping to maintain the mental health and to cultivate the spiritual resources of the community. That is one reason why monogamous marriage has the advantage over less permanent unions. It fulfils a deep need for social and religious approval as well as satisfying personal feelings. The need for religious approval is just as strong in those who are 'agin' religion as in its supporters. The 'agin religion' type is usually agin some element in traditional religion that has now served its purpose, and may express a real contact with the Spirit which is leading mankind on towards a more adequate expression of religion.

Let us look again at the ideal of monogamy and the elements involved in successful marriages.

The upholders of polygamy, whether legal as in some Eastern countries, or approximated to by men running a subsidiary 'home', usually over-stress the physical relationship and suggest that one woman cannot satisfy a man. Actually on a sheerly physical basis I believe it is the other way round, and one woman could, if she wished very rapidly exhaust a man.

However, as women develop more fully in mental and spiritual fellowship with men, and are not content simply to act as a legalised 'mistress', one woman can actually satisfy a man more adequately than several. If a man fails to be satisfied with one woman, he is not showing greater virility, *but a less mature manhood*. He is still in the infancy of the race; not having realised the true manhood involved in the dedication of the whole of his sex energies to developing an ever more satisfying and valuable partnership. Marriage is a privilege, a responsibility and an adventure simultaneously, and without all these elements it is not likely to be a successful life partnership.

The Don Juan, who prides himself on the number of sex conquests he makes little realises he is unconsciously afraid he is not man enough to satisfy any one woman adequately, and so blinds himself to his deficiencies by temporary affairs which make less demand upon him. The same principle applies to the girl out for a 'good time' at all costs, snatching at *pleasure divorced from responsibility*. This always indicates a deep though unconscious sense of inferiority and incapacity to face the real difficulties of life and to enjoy the enduring satisfaction that is only possible when responsibilities have been adequately met.

The old novels which ended 'they married and lived happily ever afterwards' give a wrong impression of marriage. Living together involves facing and adjusting to incompatibilities, and where this is recognised, a real deepening of the quality of life in both partners results. We expect from a successful marriage that there should not only be happy and contented children, but men and women who have a greater purposefulness in life, able to adjust themselves to a wider range of service to the community. Where both co-operate to face life together, neither being subservient to the other, both can develop more fully than in isolation, and the world sorely needs such happy homes. It is in unhappy homes that nervous disorders and character deficiencies develop, and make human relationships, political or international, difficult. The seeds of disease, crime and war are sown in our nurseries.

If this is to be prevented, then preparation for marriage is as important, or more important, than preparation for a professional career.

How can young people prepare for marriage today? In the first place, healthy friendships between men and women can bring an increasing understanding of the opposite sex and a greater admiration for the complementary aspects of life embodied in the other sex. The less 'possessiveness' there is in these preliminary contacts, the less is the danger of short-circuiting sexual energy on the physical level before an adequate mental and spiritual intimacy is established.

Secondly, a healthy attitude towards spontaneous stirrings of physical desire is needed. Nature will see to such relief as is necessary in sleep. But the attempt to relieve it by what for a reason I've never been able to understand are commonly called 'necking parties', actually aggravates the tension, and apart from any moral undesirability, is psychologically and physiologically bad for all parties concerned.

The child who wants to knock a nail in with a hammer soon learns that control of the hammer is essential, not only to avoid hurting his fingers but to drive the nail home. So control of our energies is essential to their adequate expression. Athletes train strenuously to achieve their skill. If it were more commonly realised that a successful marriage involves more 'skill' than any athletic championship, and is at the same time more permanently satisfying, then more men and women would qualify for happy married life and not fritter away their sexual energies on promiscuous or temporary satisfactions. Romantic love alone is not enough to make marriage a success—there must be a real compatibility of temperament and community of interest to bridge the stage when the 'halo' is seen to be in the imagination of the lover only, and the emergence of a more abiding love that is based upon real knowledge and intimacy that no longer needs the glamour of a 'halo' to maintain it.

Thirdly, there should be a full knowledge of the physical facts involved in mutual intimacy.

Lastly, there must be a genuine acceptance of the hazards and risks of life as a challenge and an opportunity. Marriages that are ways of escape from a difficult job or unhappy home on the part of the woman rarely turn out well. Neither do marriages in which the man is seeking a 'mother substitute' to look after him, instead of a wife to be a true companion. Successful living, whether married or single, requires courage, initiative and endurance. If we can achieve better relations between men and women, both in friendship and in marriage, this will in time make for healthier and happier children, and as a result a more peaceful co-operation between nations based on mutual understanding and respect.

The following example shows how a knowledge of psychology can help in resolving tensions that arise during courtship.

'You've something to do with psychology, haven't you?' asked the hairdresser who was shampooing my hair one day. On my replying that I was a psychologist, she said a little diffidently: 'Will you help me to cure my bad temper, please?'

The hairdresser's request: 'Will you help me to *cure* my bad temper?' expressed the right attitude in two ways. Bad temper does need to be cured and not punished. It is a symptom that shows all is not well with our personality and that we don't know how to handle ourselves or how to get the best out of ourselves. Secondly, the request was soundly worded. 'Will you help *me* to cure my bad temper?' This expressed a healthy sense of responsibility for its control, as well as the need for help in gaining control. No one can cure another's bad temper, control *must* come from within. But we can be helped to discover why we lose our tempers under particular conditions and so become better able to make the best of our capacities.

It is often a surprise to us to realise how much of what goes on in our minds goes on behind the scenes, so to speak. We realise the results without appreciating the underlying cause, and all attempts to deal with our personal problems without taking into account the deeper levels of mental activity which we usually refer to as 'unconscious' are inadequate. The hairdresser's case will show how control can come through gaining an insight into our real problems.

With my head in the wash-basin, I did my best to help her. Apparently her bad temper had only begun to become a nuisance recently. The girl was good-looking and intelligent. I asked her to tell me of the sort of occasions and situations in which she had actually lost her temper, and one of these in which her engagement ring 'flew off her finger accidentally' gave a clue to the trouble.

Mary had been engaged for a few months and then found herself quarrelling with her fiancé over trivial things. When they met they wasted a lot of time arguing as to what to do. If Bill wanted to go out, she would prefer something indoors. If he wanted to stay in, she would want to go out. Again and again the time in which Bill and Mary should have been enjoying doing something together was wasted, and they parted on no friendly terms.

Mary's bad temper, which also began to show with other people, had dated from this period. Eventually she admitted that she was disappointed in Bill as she got to know him better, and her temper got worse as the wedding date grew nearer. But she had not recognised the connection between this and her unconscious fear of the coming marriage.

Soon Mary realised that she had been wanting to break her engagement, but had not had the courage to admit it even to herself. She then realised the significance of her engagement ring being flung off 'accidentally' as she waved her hands in one of her outbursts, which had given me the clue as to some difficulty connected with her engagement.

I saw Mary a few times subsequently and tried to discover whether the fear of marriage was one that would have arisen *whoever* the man was, or whether it really was an expression of some deep incompatibility with Bill in particular. It is perhaps surprising to realise that there may be a real fear of marriage even when this is consciously desired and an engagement has been entered upon. Where this is general and would apply to *any* fiancé, it can usually be dispelled by a frank talk about the physical side of sex with someone who can show this is meant to be a real expression of mutual love, not *merely* a physical happening but a fulfilment of the real personality. If there has been any guilt about childish sex then this can be dispelled by realising that the grown-up expression involves a mutual relationship between man and wife, and a desire for children, so that the childish self-centredness at the back of the fear of marriage responsibilities and self-commitments can be outgrown. There is no need to go on feeling guilty about it, and the deeper our acceptance of the new venture and our self-committal to it, the more completely can childish attitudes be left behind.

However, in Mary's case, as far as it could be judged, it really did seem as if it was Bill himself who was the difficulty and that she might have been more happily engaged to a different type of man. The clash over their tastes *was* real, and she had found a touch of meanness in him that had rather horrified her. But it had not consciously entered her mind that she *could* want to go back on her word and break the engagement. Hence the outbreaks of temper which had puzzled and baffled her. She was up against a conflict in her mind between the desire to stick to her word and the dread of having to live with someone she had ceased to love, though neither side of this was really conscious, and until talking it over with me she had not realised either side of her conflicting desires. But she *was* worried at finding herself getting more and more bad tempered every day.

After Mary had realised this, she had to decide *consciously* whether there was any chance of making a successful marriage with Bill, or whether her disinclination was strong enough to make this impossible so that in fairness to Bill—as well as to herself—it would be better to break the engagement. (An engagement is just such a time for getting to know each other better with a view to seeing whether they are likely to be able to keep the solemn marriage vows 'for better for worse, in sickness or health, till death doth us part'.) When Mary realised that it would be worse to marry someone she could not make happy than to break the engagement and leave Bill free to find someone more suited to him, she decided to break the engagement. From that time her bad temper ceased.

It is worth noting that after bringing her conflict into full consciousness in this way she was able to talk it over with Bill *without* losing her temper, and found that he was actually as relieved as she was. The fault had not all been on one side, and he had been getting uneasy about the approaching wedding too.

This shows how important it is to be honest with ourselves. Mary was trying to keep her self-respect by refusing to recognise that she *could* want to break her word, when she actually *was* wanting to do so. Her temper, therefore, broke out in a way likely to lead Bill to want to get out of marrying someone who was turning into a bad-tempered girl instead of the sweet-tempered one with whom he had first fallen in love. But if the engagement had been broken in a fit of temper, as might well have happened, then neither Mary nor Bill would have been left with much respect for each other, and it would have been more difficult for either of them to find someone with whom they might have a better chance of marrying happily. The memory of the way in which their first love affair had broken down would have come in the way.

No amount of arguing with Bill could have cleared the air between them, so long as Mary was unconscious of the conflict in her own mind—between the desire to maintain her self-respect by keeping her word and her increasing reluctance to bind herself permanently in marriage to Bill. But once she had become aware of this, it was possible for her to meet the real situation intelligently and practically. Instead of the bad temper which expressed the frustration of *both* desires, there was the possibility of *action* which harmonised both. When her self-respect could be retained by meeting Bill honestly to tell him she could not see her way to making him happy, or to being happy with him, so that it would be unfair of her to go on with the engagement, the actual breaking of it satisfied both sides of the inner conflict, leaving no room for the bad temper of frustrated energies. Moreover, the genuinely difficult emotional situation was surmounted without a 'scene' such as had marred so many much more trivial occasions.

CHAPTER III

Finding the Self in Society

THE interdependence of sex, self and society is being increasingly realised. We are individual members of a large and varied human family and our needs, desires and aspirations as individuals have to be fulfilled and expressed within the framework of the 'rest of mankind', a continuing human family, through the sexual activities of the individual members of it. And as Lord Russell said in his Reith lectures, though we can destroy five hundred thousand people with a single atomic bomb, it still takes as long for human parents to produce one *new* life as it did in the Paleolithic Age. Hence the urgency of the need to harmonise the demands of sex, self and society if we are to prevent the destructive forces gaining the upper hand and putting an end to us as a race altogether.

So many false starting-points distort this close interrelation, and not only complicate life for individuals but distort the 'framework' of society within which the individual must mature, to the detriment of personal human quality and culture alike.

The nucleus of human life is not the individual but the 'family'. We so often stress the need for self-development and self-expression as if each individual was an isolated unit. Whereas we all owe our very survival to the care of parents and others during infancy, and it is within this 'social matrix' that self-consciousness emerges, not as a self in opposition to all other selves, but as *a self participating in a common family life*. Our very structure as 'potential persons' is modified by the emotional reactions and interactions of our earliest years, and the culture, whether primitive or civilised, into which we are born, is mediated through the family. We are

44

much more literally 'members one of another' than most of us realise.

There are three special stages in the development of self-consciousness and moral responsibility. The first occurs in early years when the baby begins to refer to himself as 'I' instead of 'baby'. There has been an *integration* of sensations, emotions and impulses which are held together within a focus of self-consciousness that differentiates itself from the external world and from other selves. Self-assertion, so often called naughtiness, is a necessary stage in the process of differentiating each self from other selves. If this is accepted within a family circle that can call out sufficient loyalty to the 'whole' to lead to a healthy give and take between its members, self-consciousness can develop normally and the basis for a stable and co-operative individual is effected.

Where, however, self-assertion is looked upon as 'original sin' that must be exorcised at all costs, then the process of self-development is twisted and thwarted, and the rebel or the neurotic may result. The conflict in the child mind can be very intense, with its great need for love and security as well as for self-expression.

If, in an attempt to satisfy a parental demand to be good, self-assertive tendencies that are essential to healthy development are repressed, neurosis in later life is inevitable. Yet unless these can be modified within the give and take of healthy family life, so that affection can hold the balance between the demands and clamours for self-expression amongst its various members, the foundation for the rebel, revolutionary or delinquent always 'up agin' society and authority, is laid.

There has been a reaction from the authoritarian 'find out what Tommy is doing and tell him not to' to discovering the real needs of a growing child mind if it is to grow up capable of genuine loyalty and co-operation. But it is perhaps important to stress that this does not involve merely letting a child have its own way. A child does need help in gaining control over its own at first conflicting impulses. But it must be the help of sufficient security and affection within which to experiment without being made to feel guilty or ashamed of natural impulses in themselves. The importance of a genuine balance between the fundamental needs for affection, significance and security within the family circle in establishing a real focus of self-consciousness rightly orientated towards other selves in this first *integration* of self, cannot be over-emphasised. If this is healthily established, growth and development can lead to increasing fullness of life and zest for living, to the benefit of the individual and society. Where it is distorted by the failure of the environment to provide sufficient security and affection, then later development is painful and distressing both to the individual and the community. *Unfortunately the individual usually gets the blame.*

A second stage in the development of the ego occurs during adolescence. Here again there is a further *integration* of the various drives and impulses which express the awakening of sex and awareness of society. Here, if the first stage in childhood has been satisfactorily effected, the second stage in adolescence has a better chance of succeeding in the always difficult balance between individual desires and social demands and opportunities.

Again, however, social influence plays a very large part in helping or hindering the growth and harmonisation of impulses within the individual that can further the development of society or cut across it. If through the interactions of the growing self and the milieu in which it comes to awareness of its capacities with their responsibilities, and also of its limitations, there is sufficient *love* to balance the needs of the individual with loyalty to the community, the good citizen can emerge, able to make his or her contribution to the well-being of the whole. If the difficulties the adolescent has with himself, which *are* accentuated by *the many past failures of adaptation and adjustment in the history of the race*, which have left their traces in each of us, are treated as culpable, his development is made unnecessarily painful and the finding of his real niche in society may be long delayed—to the loss of both the individual and the community.

But, whether these two expanding stages are passed through satisfactorily or not, nature does not allow us to rest content with any achievement. Middle-age brings with it the need for a *third* re-orientation of self, sex and society. So far, few seem to have realised this and the wreckage of lives unable to find the way to or through the third stage of the human life-cycle is far greater than is usually realised. Moreover, the repercussions of this within society, wherein effective control of policy is more in the hands of the middle-aged or elderly, many of whom have never 'grown up' to maturity, than in that of youth, are often disastrous.

We provide Child Guidance Clinics for maladjusted children: we provide special approved schools or Borstal Institutions for the difficult adolescent. But we make no provision for the 'middle-aged' who find the burden of life increasing more rapidly than they can keep pace with it. If these break down they *may* get help through a psychologist, or even in a mental hospital, if the breakdown goes as far as that. But the thousands who could be helped to avoid breakdown and to play a genuinely responsible and creative part in the life of the community do not know where to turn for help and advice. The majority probably do not even know there *is* the possibility of a third phase with the *reinforcement of nature behind it.* As one woman said, 'I can just see myself going on doing the same thing and getting crabbier and crabbier over it as I get older,' instead of seeing the possibility of the continuing adventure that can transfigure the really mature right onto old age itself.

It is significant that Christ at the age of 30, which in the East, with its more rapid maturing, would be the equivalent of our middle age, went through an apparently critical re-orientation in the Wilderness, after which He began His public ministry, speaking with authority and not as the scribes. This maturing of personality on a higher level dynamically related to the cosmical and not merely the tribal background of life, brought Him into conflict with the narrower loyalties of the day. Nevertheless, the abiding influence of His life and death would seem from another angle to endorse the validity of the insights into reality and the effectiveness of such an integration as *a genuine third stage in the process of the maturation of personality*. His call to others to follow suit and be 'born again' not of the will of man (society), nor of the flesh (sex), but of the Spirit, would seem to indicate this as a fulfilment and not a destroyal of the preceding stages, and as a *norm* for mature Christian living.

It is for those 'middle-aged folk' whose middle-aged spread is extending to their minds as well as their bodies, that this book is primarily written. The interrelatedness of the various stages in life is indicated. The problems of youth, courtship and marriage through which they have passed, well or ill, are outlined, and the possibility of utilising even their own failures on these levels constructively and so winning a maturity that can be personally satisfying, socially useful and a fulfilment and not a negation of their own youth, is opened up to them. Here in this third phase of our development as 'persons within a community' lies the completion of the first two in infancy and adolescence. The matured individual pours back into the community all that has been mediated to him through the community in his early years that he has been able to assimilate. The pull of sex, self and society, so often in opposition in childhood and adolescence, as well as in early married life, *can* now find a harmonisation that is free from egotism, free from sexual antagonisms or indulgences, capable of responsible relations with either sex, and a deeper love for husband, wife or children than was possible in the earlier periods. Sex, self and society are here harmonised by loyalty to the 'communion of saints' of all ages, races and peoples, whose culture has enriched their own heritage sufficiently for them to carry the torch on to the next generation, enriching the cultural life of the specific community within which they live. Unless youth has such a cultural background mediated through the more mature, its tensions and rivalries *cannot* be adequately resolved, and these embitter and disrupt personal, social and political life.

So to the middle aged, who thought life had no more to offer, comes the great challenge in these days of crises, in this 'age between the ages', with one civilisation and culture dying and the new, apparently powerless to come to birth, a challenge to play our part in making it possible for our children's children to enter into the heritage it falls to us to *prepare*.

But if we are to do this, our roots must go deeply into the eternal ground of our life, or we will only perpetuate our own weaknesses. The call is to deepen and purify our religious experience, trusting God to complete that which He has begun.

'Work out your own salvation in fear and trembling, for it is God who worketh in *you*.'

CHAPTER IV

Youth and Middle Age

YOUTH and middle age have one thing in common, both the adolescent entering into a wider world through the rapid development of his energies, and the middle aged *finding the idealism of youth in conflict with frustrating realities*, are problems for themselves. Childhood and old age have their own problems, but these are predominantly problems for others, not for themselves. The parent of a problem child has to take the responsibility for trying to help the child to face its difficulties: the relatives of the aged have to become responsible for protecting them from the full force of problems beyond their power to meet. 'Second childhood' is a problem for the relatives, not for the elderly child.

Whereas in adolescence and middle age the onus for facing problems lies with the individual who achieves maturity in proportion as he faces the task of adjusting to life as a whole, including in this adjustment to his or her own forces, to society, to the opposite sex, and to the unseen background of life which is religious.

Before going on to the specific problems which face the adolescent and the middle aged respectively, it is helpful to consider the religious background within which these specific problems can best be faced. I do not mean any particular denomination, but the relation of the individual to God which may be mediated through many forms and cultures.

In early childhood emphasis should be on God the Father: a kindly Providence giving a sense of security and freedom, mediated through the love and care of parents who neither 'spoil' the child nor 'condemn' his childish maladjustments as dreadful wickedness. It cannot be too strongly stressed that the conception of God mediated through the reality of the *life* of parents or guardians is responsible for a great deal of the health and stability, or for the disease or instability of the adolescent or middle aged. The foundation for 'knowing God' is laid in childhood, and the child's spontaneous recognition of the hidden godhead in many of the natural joys of life sternly repressed by ascetism should not be quenched if a normal religious development is to follow. Childhood's prayers must be the prayers of a child, not an attempt to make children pray like imitation grown-ups.

When we come to adolescence, with the phase in which the child begins to feel a real sense of responsibility struggling with an inadequate capacity for control, the emphasis of religious teaching should be on God the Son—adolescence is the age of idealism, of hero-worship, of the formation of sentiments of loyalty. The historic Christ here is the form through which God can most fruitfully impress Himself on, and gain the worship of, the adolescent. It is just here so many mistakes in the teaching of religion have been made. To extend and emphasise God as Father, stressing the authoritarian aspect, is either to create the rebel who throws over religion or to stifle the growing independence of the adolescent as he seeks to become 'himself', a real individual and not just an undifferentiated replica of his parents. Here the emphasis on the Person of Christ is a healthy and essential background to the adolescent's difficult task in outgrowing childishness and becoming a responsible human being. It serves to focus the idealism so prominent in the first flowering of wider capacities, intellectual, aesthetic and moral, in a 'Hero' who lived under similar difficulties and so, if rightly presented, can keep this idealism in relation to the realities of life, and not let it spend itself in *dreaming* of a better world instead of *living* in this one so as to get the best out of it and put the best we can into it. The many-sidedness of the still youthful 'historic Jesus' needs to be emphasised, not a meek and mild fantasy Christ. No meek and mild Christ would have been dynamic enough to get Himself crucified. Jesus combined so many paradoxes. He was tender as a woman with those in distress, and stern and relentless with those who were self-satisfied. He was solitary in His communing with God in His early-morning prayers—yet fulfilled his duties in the synagogue. He called His followers to sacrifice all earthly attachments and risk death itself to be true to Him, yet He was open to the gibe of being a glutton and a wine-bibber, because He blessed and enjoyed the normal social life around Him, not repudiating it with the false asceticism of so many of His followers.

Here is an ideal to which youth can respond. On learning to say 'Our Father' with Christ, the adolescent passes beyond the complete dependence of childhood and begins to grow into the sonship which, like that of Christ, can express and carry out some *specific* part of the purpose of God on earth. God is still Father—but the emphasis in adolescence is on the sonship of man, as self-consciousness emerges as the heritage and responsibility of manhood and womanhood, through which the life of instinct has to be 'baptised into Christ'.

Emphasis on the historic Christ also serves to focus the spirit of adventure so strong in the normal healthy adolescent. If this is lacking, we know repression has been at work, distorting and stunting life. The fear of the middle-aged parent who tries to curb the growing spirit of youth is an expression of a frustrated youth itself, seeking to prevent others from going beyond them and so revealing the sham expressed in their own narrow respectability.

Then during maturity and passing on to middle age, if the foundation of the religious life has been truly laid in the child's awareness of, and dependence upon, God the Father, and the adolescent's worship of the Hero Christ, in whose service he finds freedom, the third era can come into being—the era of the Holy Spirit. Here the emphasis should be on the indwelling Spirit of Christ in man. Christ in *us* the hope of glory. We no longer seek to serve an external Christ of 2000 years ago. We find ourselves responding to the living Presence of Christ in us. The problem for maturity and middle age is this deepening of the inner life so that God may act more directly through our own insight and initiative than He can do through the hero worship of youth, which always, even when hero worship of the Christ, *tends to idealise its object*. In maturity our ideals have to be brought into relation to the real possibilities open to us, and the truly creative phase of life begins as we find just where and how we can pull our weight in the great scheme of things, *accepting limitations that youth tends to repudiate*, as the very means through which the purpose of God is incarnated, is carried forward on earth.

But here the unity of God is made most manifest. It is not three separate Gods who govern childhood, youth and maturity. It is the one God revealing that aspect of Himself which will best meet the needs of a humanity with a long period of infancy and adolescence. Just as the child who has found security and freedom in the loving all-seeing, all-knowing Father, and not the fear of the all-seeing, all-condemning bogy some parents substitute for God, can best grow into the comradeship with Christ that makes for a healthy adolescence, pruning the exuberance of youthful imagination by its contact with life: so the person on the brink of maturity, who has gained as a permanent possession this awareness of the Father's care and the focussing of ideals in the historic Christ, is equipped for the phase of the indwelling spirit, and armed against the many religious vagaries of the middle-aged spiritual valetudinarian, seeking in various cults the *life he has failed to cultivate in himself*.

We see these three phases exemplified in the Bible itself. In the childhood of the Jews we get God the Father—in the first three Gospels we get God the Son, the focussing point for adolescent humanity, in its transition from a religion projected into the heavens to a kingdom of heaven in the heart of man. While in St. John's Gospel and parts of the Pauline epistles we find the *religion of maturity* expressed in the indwelling spirit of the Christ of the gospels *in every man*. The historic Christ has mediated the Universal Christ to man and so revealed the Father as incarnate in the Son and through Him in all who make the life of Christ their own. So the Divine spark of life in man goes through its cycle from the depths of the Unconscious whence it is projected on to the material Universe, through the focus of the Person of Christ, to the bridging of the gulf between conscious and unconscious in the maturity of Christian personality, which incarnates or embodies the eternal spirit of Christ within it.

So far few seem to have trodden the last lap of their cycle— the majority, even amongst Christians, have remained on the level of childish or adolescent religion. The last war, breaking out twenty years after a war to end war, is a challenge to us to grow up and respond to the Spirit of Christ within us, which alone can be creative enough to bring a new world order into being through the death of the old one. We too may find the power of His resurrection if we share the cruci-fixions of the present time in His Spirit, extending thus, as St. Paul put it, the sufferings of Christ for His Body's sake, which is the Church.

But if we are to do this we must take very seriously the *problems of youth*. We must seek to let them develop so as to become the kind of people when mature that we should have been had we not clung to the past instead of going forward towards the future, so that they may build the better world we shall not live to see ourselves. And if we can do this, sacrificing our thought for ourselves *to bring youth towards the maturity that we cannot now achieve ourselves*, we too shall find something of the peace of God which passes under-standing and find we are doing the one thing left to us to do that *can* serve the purpose of God in spite of our failure, and so losing our lives, we too shall find them in the kingdom that is to be.

Now to come to the special problems of youth. During adolescence there is a rapid though somewhat unequal expansion in many directions. This makes for a disproportionate growth, mentally, physically and emotionally, which is often the despair of the adolescent, and unless it is understood, of parents, teachers and guardians.

The very facts of rapid and disproportionate physical growth alone can cause great distress to the youth who finds hands, feet and nose unduly prominent, and who at the same time is always being scolded for being clumsy, when actually he may be doing his best to co-ordinate movements whose previous balance has been thrown out of gear by this disproportionate growth. Anyone who has tried to walk upstairs with shoes too large for him, and finds himself catching the extra long toe on almost every step because he cannot gauge how much to allow for it, can sympathise with and understand this. A little encouragement to the awkward, self-conscious youth who does not know what to do with his hands or feet can help him to realise this is a passing phase and help him to gain control more quickly through the confidence that springs from a knowledge that the easy movements of those he envies *have also been gained through such awkward stages.* The assurance this brings aids in co-ordinating movements as surely as the sense of inferiority about it impedes it and makes the period of temporary awkwardness a long-drawn-out agony. Many of the undesirable compensations for this 'natural' ungainliness can be avoided by helping boys and girls in their teens in this way. The old fashion of squashing feet into narrow, pointed toes, a fashion followed by the youth of both sexes, and on all except the very lowest poverty level, was an unhealthy reaction to this feeling of being ashamed of the size of their feet—and many foot troubles in later life which prevent full health of body result from this misguided youthful vanity—a vanity that often persists beyond adolescence because never faced and understood then.

The late Dr. Ikin, in his book on Religious Instruction, quotes some examples of youthful reactions to bodily growth. A fourteen-year-old boy took to tiptoeing all the time. When his annoyed mother questioned him he became sullen, but sympathetic questioning elicited the fact that he tiptoed for fear of making too much noise with 'such beastly large shoes'.

A girl of fifteen constantly assumed a semi-crouching posture when with groups of people by bending her knees. Psychological examination discovered that the girl thus sought to seem 'smaller' because she 'simply could not stand to be so awfully tall'.

Another girl refused to attend church because her 'neck felt so long in church with everyone looking at it'.

In all these cases, had there been understanding and *informed* parents aware of these difficulties, the *self-consciousness of which these actions were symptoms* could have been avoided. Parents must learn to anticipate such difficulties and help adolescents to laugh off their awkwardness as temporary, instead of compensating for it in phantasies of superiority out of relation to any of their real capacities.

The difference between phantasies and ideals is of the utmost importance for character development. Ideals must be in harmony with our capacities, though expressing them on a level beyond that of present achievement, then they spur us on to outgrow our present state and achieve a better. Fresh ideals, still related to capacities and opportunities, can then emerge, so that the goal is still ahead and not behind. When ideals and capacities (or incapacities) are not related, then phantasies flourish. These, instead of preparing us for grown-up life, sap the energy which should be going into emotional relationships and strengthening group loyalties. The life of phantasy in which every boy is hero and every girl heroine compensates in imagination and not in reality for the difficulties of adaptation to a rapidly expanding world with rapidly expanding but inco-ordinated powers. But wherever this develops sufficiently to be a danger to the individual, leading him further from reality and from the social contacts that alone can counteract the self-consciousness which gives rise to phantasy compensations, there *someone in authority is always partly to blame.* You will notice I said 'wherever this develops sufficiently to be a danger'. As with children, so with adolescents, a certain amount of phantasying is normal and helpful —it is only where this becomes a *substitute* for living that it is dangerous and can eventually lead to the mental hospital as a case of dementia praecox or schizophrenia. The trouble with the dangerous type of phantasy is that the boy or girl identifies himself with the phantasied self and so puts an end to any effort to bridge the gulf between an ego-ideal or ideal self and the present self. This identification comes because he cannot accept the reality of the limitations and imperfections which are there. And this implies some grown-up person has made him feel unloved and disliked to an unbearable degree for it. Just as we find in Child Guidance Clinics it is so often the parents who needed the guidance, and for whose failures the children are suffering: so with adolescents who fail to progress and turn away from reality as beyond their capacity to face, we find parents, teachers, guardians or religious teaching has blocked the way—*and it is unfortunate that it is the adolescent who ends in an institution, and not those who drove him into his regressive life,* whether of delinquency or insanity. There was a considerable increase in juvenile delinquency when children born during the First World War reached adolescence, and a similar increase of dementia praecox in youths between twenty and twenty-five was noted just before the last war. The instability of home life during the first war seemed to have had its effect on some of those possibly not too well equipped to meet it owing to malnutrition, and the fear and anxiety which may have accompanied their birth. We must see to it that more understanding help is given to adolescents in future if we would prevent a similar increase of serious emotional failure after the last war. There *has* been a similar increase in juvenile delinquency since the war, which is likely to increase for a time. Can we prevent still more serious disturbances?

Adolescence is the period when consciousness of self is growing, when moral responsibility is increasing, when mental life is developing but experience is very limited. Intelligence reaches its maximum during adolescence—reasoning powers and the capacity for abstract thought show themselves then and the level is rarely passed in later life—the gain in thinking power in maturity comes not from greater intelligence, but from *a wider experience of life and a more balanced emotional life*. It is therefore natural that the problem of self-consciousness is acute for the adolescent. He must learn to differentiate himself from his parents, society, etc., if he is to grow up into a morally responsible being. Many of the things for which he is blamed by teacher or parents are not the signs of original sin they are so often taken to be, but of *original righteousness which will out in spite of* the repressive effects of parents and teachers.

Adolescence is the time when independence is to be achieved. If this struggle to assert the life that is in him over against a pattern imposed from without is taken to be wickedness and the individual is estranged from authority in the process, authority wrongly used is to blame for the rebel that results, instead of the reliable and responsible person who has succeeded *in becoming himself*. Parents need a great deal of help in learning how they may foster this spirit of independence in ways that make for greater social service and a more fully personal spiritual life if they are to avoid trying to compress youth into their own mould. We shall deal later with some of the difficulties of the parent who has remained adolescent at heart and who refuses to allow his children to grow up because he cannot admit his failure to do so himself, therefore at all cost the children must not surpass him or he might begin to realise all was not well with himself. Talks for parents side by side with talks for youth are essential. We've got to admit such a *large-scale failure* that individual methods are not sufficient—if we are to help youth to grow towards a more wholesome maturity, we must help parents to realise the necessity for surpassing themselves, or youth will merely *revolt against the old without gaining the power to create anything better in the new world it seeks.* It is on the basis of fellowship and not of self-assertion that the new order must be built, and for this co-operation between young and old is necessary. But it must *be co-operation*, a real realisation that each has something to give and not the domination of either one by the other.

The problem of the nature of society is very prominent in the adolescent—public school and factory alike. The healthy adolescent finds himself in a world of great values and great injustices, and urgently desires to improve it. His methods may be on wrong lines owing to lack of experience, but his energy is undoubted and it is for those who are more mature to encourage these efforts on constructive lines. The old die-hard attitude of 'what was good enough for our fathers is good enough for us' is shattered. One 'war to end war' might allow it to persist in the most die-hard. But another in our own lifetime must shatter it for all except those so sure they only are right as to be insane—whether certified or not.

So let us help youth through its personal conflicts to become the kind of people who may succeed where we middle-aged folk have failed—only so can there be hope for the world regeneration so sorely needed.

In addition to a fuller recognition of society and the ability to think and plan and criticise, the adolescent who passed the mental age of twelve begins to want some comprehensive scheme of the universe. He wants to understand how things come to be as they are. His range of insight may be great or small, but his moral questionings baffle and frequently embarrass the middle-aged parents who have stifled their own search for a fuller life and settled down to accept things as they are. Adolescents are often shocked at the compromises with conscience middle age sometimes perpetrates. And adolescents are also shocked by the apparent dullness of middle-aged imagination, they certainly don't want to grow up like that! If older people realised this it would benefit both. As it is, older people tend to try to mould young ones into youthful editions of themselves, having failed to grow up with the youthfulness that accompanies creative people right on to old age itself.

Again in connection with sex, youth is in a transition period. After a latent period, with little sex curiosity, comes the development of the physical sex organs and many secondary changes due to the activity of sex glands occur. Boys and girls become aware of each other in a new way. If in childhood they have been enlightened by wise parents and natural curiosity satisfied, this *awakening of interest will always have something of reverence in it that can never be wholly lost.* If on the other hand their natural curiosity has been put off with untrue stories and they have been made to feel sex is indecent—then this awakening of interest and greater awareness of physical needs can cause a great conflict between it and the idealism of youth—to be ashamed, in spite of one's self, of one's desires in the presence of someone who attracts him, is a curse far too often laid on youth by parents who thought they were protecting his 'innocence' and were actually making innocence impossible. A good deal of adolescent masturbation results from this difficulty of bringing together the more physical aspects of sex with the emotional attraction felt for some one girl who stands out from the rest as ideal, and this need never have been had not the parents projected their own guilty attitude onto sex itself and so robbed their children of their spiritual heritage.

One of the greatest needs of youth if it is to grow towards a wholesome maturity, able to carry the culture of the race a stage further than before is *an understanding attitude on the part of all in authority to the problems facing youth today.*

There is an interesting period just before puberty which seems to be a recapitulation of the level of maturity of a more primitive humanity. Stanley Hall, in his monumental work on adolescence, points out that the emphasis in play at this period 'seem to be of savage out-door life—hunting, fishing, stealing, swimming, rowing, sailing, fighting, hero-worship, adventure'.[1] It is important to realise this as the standards of value, moral as well as aesthetic, belong more nearly to this more primitive social level than to our modern world. Many juvenile delinquents arise because of the clash between rules or laws they may understand and recognise are imposed on them, *while the emotional drive or feeling which would give them the power to respond is still focussed on the more primitive* level. It is often here not a matter of original sin or depravity, but of a difficulty in passing from one level of culture to another. This may perhaps be best illustrated by the fact that 97·7 per cent. of indictable offences amongst juveniles below the age of 17 are offences against property, and the age at which this is at its peak is 13 (for boys). (The problem of juvenile delinquency is mainly one amongst boys. In 1938 the number of girls under 17 found guilty of indictable offences was 1,747 as opposed to 26,369 for boys.) (The peak age for girls is 19, not 13.)

It is obvious here that one major problem of youth concerns the attitude to property. Our very complicated system of property, of 'having, sanctioned by law', as Miss Fry in the fifth Clarke Hall lecture described it, seems beyond the

Stanley Hall, *Adolescence.*

capacity of many youthful people to grasp. If we realised this, we might do much to help the pre-adolescent to affect this transition from the values of one cultural level to another *before* he has to face the physical, mental and emotional changes of adolescence itself. It is perhaps worth emphasising that the juvenile delinquent does not inevitably become the confirmed criminal. The peak age for indictable offences for all age-groups is at 13 for boys and 19 for girls—after adolescence there is a continuous and steadily falling off of indictable offences. So help brought to bear at this time may reduce the problem of delinquency considerably. This is the period when 'gangs' are formed. A great deal depends on the kind of 'gang' available. The Scout movement is a splendid way of training this gang loyalty so that it may eventually lead to responsible citizenship. The genius of Baden-Powell saw the need for youth to live out this phase of adventure seeking primitive life *with the approval of authority instead of in defiance of it*. The immediate success of the movement inevitably led to the development of Guides to provide a similar training for girls. The need, however, does not seem to be as urgent for girls as in the case of boys. This provides a splendid opportunity for socialising adolescents and helping them to become responsible citizens, valuing skill and knowledge and discipline. The more recent 'Outward Bound' movement is another extension of this principle.

Where these opportunities are not available, then there is the tendency for 'gangs' *agin authority* to be formed, often basing themselves on the desperado gangster type of film: conflict with authority inevitably widens the gulf between their standards of right and wrong and those of the community, setting them more firmly in opposition to authority. Great wisdom is needed in dealing with such youthful delinquents if they are to be helped to grow up into useful citizens. If they can be won over they might actually find their best sphere of work amongst the police who were at one time their 'hereditary enemies', supporting law with the same energy that previously led them to rebel against it as meaningless, soft or unmanly.

This brings us to another problem of youth, namely that of deciding in what way they are to earn their living. The choice of the nature of work or a career is of the utmost importance. So often the choice is dictated by the parent and is not in accordance with the capacities of the boy or girl. Temperamental factors as well as the level of intelligence and opportunities for training should be borne in mind. For example, in one factory where the welfare worker applied some quite elementary temperament tests she reduced the labour turnover to a quarter of what it had been as the girls were more contented with work that suited them. Many problems in later life arise through misfits in work who cannot find satisfactory sublimations of their instinctive energies along the lines chosen for them—office work does not provide as suitable a channel for the sublimations of a strong maternal instinct as nursing, for example—and typists or clerks may make unsatisfactory marriages as a way of escape from this. On the other hand, women whose maternal instinct is weak do not as a rule make good nurses. A more impersonal form of work in office, shop or factory is more satisfactory. In the same way a boy with a strong bent for adventure is not likely to make a good bank clerk, but may make a very good sailor.

The importance of vocational guidance for the future mental health and social usefulness of the individual cannot be overstressed. Here too is room for pastoral work. Some talks to parents should be given in every parish, or by local education authorities, outlining some of the principles that can help them to guide their children wisely in this choice, only second in importance to the wise choice of a marriage partner. This is true on all levels of society, except possibly the real slum, which is in any case an environment to be abolished at all costs as soon as possible. The illustration from one factory shows that variety is available amongst work ranked as socially and economically equal. The problem reaches its climax, however, amongst the youth from professional homes, who naturally aim at a professional career—the doctor who is determined his artistic son shall become a doctor and follow on with his practice may lead to a very unsatisfied or frustrated doctor, never really making good at it, out of a boy who might have had a satisfactory and useful career as an architect. So too the ambition of clergy to have sons who will in turn join the ministry is not always wise. There are still too many clergy struggling bravely to fulfil a vocation for which they are not fitted. Some through their own mistaken choice, others through filial loyalty following a father's choice, until too late to follow their real bent in some other direction.

This brings us to one other point which should be stressed with regard to religious education. Amongst the more educated youth, with a knowledge of evolution, there is very frequently a conflict between their knowledge of biological facts and religion as so often presented to them. Dr. Olive Wheeler in *Youth* states that 47 per cent. of a student group were obsessed by doubts of this kind for a period of years. Dr. Wheeler couples this with the conflict sometimes expressed as between 'God is love' and 'Falling in love' and curiosity concerning the facts of life. She then goes on to say, 'there is surely something amiss where parents and educators of adolescents fail to minister to, or to take into account this curiosity, and when spiritual leaders so tend to sectionalise experience into the secular and the sacred, and to keep in separate compartments their biology and their theology, that they fail to give effective help in solving the greatest conflict of adolescence'.[1]

Lastly, it is important that while we help the adolescent all we can we should not impress our own adult views on him.

[1] *Youth*, p. 170.

If the individual's religion is to be his own *it must grow from within.* We need more *faith in the power of God to appeal directly to youth through the spiritual universe to which he is so supremely capable of responding,* and less faith in our own *partial* interpretation of Reality if youth is to become able to carry the torch of the spirit beyond the level we ourselves have succeded in keeping it alight.

This leads us on, naturally, to the problems of the middle aged which form the subject of the next chapter, as this actually constitutes one of the very real problems for the middle-aged, namely *how to adjust the balance between authority and freedom, how to unite a reverence for and respect of tradition with the power to live creatively, adjusting to ever more finely discriminated cultural ideals.* If the religion of youth is to grow from within, it is essential that youth be provided with the right environment and given the material from which its conclusions can be drawn. Nothing less than the religious orientation of the whole educational system and the life of both home and school can provide the right environment within which youth can solve its problems constructively and grow freely towards a maturity that is creative and not on the defensive.

The separation between the secular and the religious aspects of life in our times has led to a Western civilisation at war with itself. Until we can re-unite what God has joined together, so long will the problems of youth and middle age alike involve a stress and a suffering *that is not inherent in the process of transition* but brought upon us by the *artificial splitting of our life.* It is significant that more of the inmates of mental hospitals are schizophrenics—those of 'split minds'— than any other type of mental disorder. If when we come to the problems of the middle aged we can begin to close the gulf between religion as conceived and life as lived, we shall also be helping to solve the problems of youth that we failed to solve in our own youth and reach a measure of real maturity.

CHAPTER V

Psychological Problems of Maturity

WHERE the problems of childhood and adolescence have been lived through without undue repression or distortion, middle age may make a *deepening of the spiritual life* possible. The normal goals of a career, marriage and parenthood occupy the period following adolescence. Adaptation to work, to society and to love have been effected. Children, where there have been any, are growing up and are usually independent or nearly so. What then is left for the middle aged? Is life to grow steadily less worth while with less zest and to lead to a fixation which prevents growth, or is it to open out to a fuller life of the mind and spirit as lessening physical energies makes competition with the activities of the younger generation difficult? It is a crucial phase, and whether we have a deepening life making its contribution to the culture of the community by its *poise, balance and increasing wisdom*, or whether we have an increasingly neurotic old age wrapped up in self-concern and alienating instead of inspiring the younger generation is really the difference between spiritual life and death. It matters supremely not only to the individual but to the *community* which attitude is adopted. We hear much of the problems of childhood and adolescence, but very little as yet about the problems of middle age, which are quite as far reaching and important as those of any of the critical periods of life. Much less help is available at this period and much unnecessary suffering is caused through ignorance and the lack of any guidance as to how to adjust to the changes involved. The change of course is far more marked and critical with women than with men. The far-reaching glandular changes accompanying the climacteric are one factor influencing this, moreover there is a greater change for the married woman when children no longer need so much time and care than for the man whose main work continues as a rule for a long time beyond the period of middle age. Some factors, however, are common to both, and the time to prevent the fairly frequent nervous breakdowns when business men retire is to *face the problems of middle age constructively*. For both sexes there should be the recognition of a slowing down of physical activity and the acceptance of other aims and goals. Jung has suggested that if the first half of life serves the purpose of procreation, the care of the family, and the active work to maintain it, *the purpose of the second half of life may be to develop and maintain culture.* He said that if there was nothing more to be achieved after middle age, then men and women would not be allowed by nature to live beyond it as they do, and this achievement can only be a *cultural* aim. True culture springs from within and depends upon a realisation of inner values. Good manners that are only skin deep cannot be creative of the cultured attitude which springs spontaneously from the integrated personality. Thus the major task for the middle aged is the deepening of their own inner life, the cultivation of the garden of the spirit. This is very different from the neurotic pre-occupation with themselves that springs from their refusal to let go the outer activities and power goals of earlier ambitions. The latter, which no longer can compete on even terms with the natural 'will to power' of youth, evades its real responsibilities and seeks power as an end. The normal 'will to power' of healthy ambition *desires power to achieve some end and to be effective must be socially useful.* The perverted 'will to power' of the middle-aged neurotic who may terrorise over the home, the hospital, the office or even a nation—if a nation succumbs to a similar fixation—seeks power to compensate for inner weakness. Power which is an end in itself and not merely a means loses its contact with real forces and sooner or later finds itself bankrupt, a blind drive which has lost all purpose and cannot satisfy either the individual who has sought it blindly or the community within which its destructive effects are expressed. This is the way of losing one's life by seeking it. Whereas the only effective way of gaining one's inner life is by losing external attachments *when they have served their purpose*, allowing fresh goals in contact with reality to emerge.

The number of disillusioned, frustrated middle-aged people who eventually become a drag on all around them as they grow to an old age which is clinging to the past instead of still looking forward is a heavy indictment of our Western culture. We have made it hard for individuals to find *their own true line of development* which would have deepened our culture. We have so stressed efficiency and activity that weary middle-aged women have their faces lifted to smooth out wrinkles which need not have been there because they cannot get employment if they look their age. While in trying to maintain the standard of youth throughout middle age they fail to achieve the inner harmony and poise that would help both old and young and bring poise and balance into the community which civilisation, in danger through warfare such as is increasingly widespread in this century, so sorely needs if our excessive activity is not to undermine its very possibility. The emphasis in the second half of life should be on *being*, but we find today so often youth seeks to guide without the wisdom of assimilated experience because middle age clings to the activities of youth and refuses to become the inspiration of the young, and the vicious circle goes on.

Dr. William Brown gave a paper on the problems of maturity at an International Congress of Medical Psychology at Oxford. I think if we could adopt that term instead of problems of middle-age we would find the sense of *depreciation* so often implied in 'middle-age' would not be aroused and the *positive aim* would be emphasised.

Now what are these problems? Dr. William Brown points

out that in the late forties or early fifties the ethical demands upon both men and women are very great. The individual, he says, is called upon to abandon the last vestiges of Narcissism, or 'self-love', to devote himself without the slightest reservation to the Christian ideal—indeed the noblest pagan idea also—of the surrendered life, of giving up in order that he may be more efficient on the spiritual plane, of losing his life that he may find it. Jung points out that whilst in the first half we are preparing for life, in the latter half we are preparing for death. The eternal transcendant element implicit in all human experience should become more explicit as we face the *climax of physical and mental expansion.* In so far as we respond to this, we find a deeper significance in the experiences through which we have *already* lived and life becomes *more*, not less, worth while. For Jung the purpose of 'individuation', the making whole of the personality by including the apparently less desirable aspects of it and redeeming—or, as he puts it, Christianising—it, is the major task of middle age. Neuroses after thirty-five years of age are always fundamentally religious problems. The patients have either not been able to keep their contact with or awareness of the deep abiding spiritual realities inherent in their experience, or have never become aware of them. In either case the individual so maimed finds life too much for him and turns in upon himself to escape the demands of life, becoming a burden to himself and to the community. The cure demands a very different type of introversion. Instead of a turning in on oneself, short-circuiting psychic energy in ego fantasies, *a deliberate purposive introversion must be faced to get into touch with the lost forces of the soul through which alone the power to rise to the challenge of life can come.* As Jung points out, with the purposiveness outreaching human ends, neurosis dies and moral progress can begin.

The moral problems involved in the difficulties of the middle aged are a real challenge, and the way in which these difficulties are faced and solved is vital to culture and Christianity itself. Every adequate solution of mental conflict or moral problem extends the range of insight and opens the way to a further set of problems. *To be psychologically healthy does not mean to be free from problems.* That is rather a condition of psychological idiocy; but it means to have a *creative attitude* towards the problems that arise, so that each one solved leads on to the emergence of another. Moreover, *no* psychological problem can be solved merely by thinking about it. Adequate solutions are the result of *living* creatively and *our periods of most acute distress may yield us the richest blessings in character.* One thing here must be borne in mind, and that is that the turmoil and stress that may be involved in this period can be very greatly enhanced by the failure to have overcome the difficulties of either childhood or adolescence. Where there has been a disturbance which has not been put right in these earlier periods, it may be necessary to seek the help of a medical psychologist in order to get through this period. If this is done not merely with a view to getting through as easily as possible, but with the *real intention of making a better job of the last half of life than one has done of the first*, the process, though more painful than when free from early complications, can still work its way out to a synthesis of *abiding value* and harmony well worth the suffering involved in facing up to the past failures and not running away from them. The need for people who can give wise advice and help during this period will be obvious. *The gain to the whole community if problems at this time could be so faced as to prevent the carry-over of infantile attitudes into old age would revolutionise our whole society.*

Now let us consider in more detail some of the particular difficulties that arise during middle age. One fairly common one is dissatisfaction with the kind of work being done. When the choice of one profession has been made it has often been at the expense of other interests. For example, someone may hesitate whether to take up music as a career or to keep it as a hobby and teach some other subject or to go into business. During the period of expanding activity all may go well: then either the work tends to become mere routine, requiring less libido [1] to fulfil it, and the desire for the joys of the career discarded may loom large; or with waning physical energies the actual difficulties loom larger and again the pull of the previously rejected choice makes itself strongly felt. It is a help to many to know how common this is and it may prevent the throwing over of the chosen career in favour of one which is now actually beyond their powers, since to be successful it should have been followed at the start. Unless the position is faced squarely, there may be a very rapid decrease of efficiency, as the belief that a wrong choice has been made tends to diminish self-confidence; and to compensate for this inefficiency, phantastic estimates of what one would have achieved on the other line may still further alienate the mind from reality until a serious breakdown occurs.

Even clergy are not immune from this kind of problem. The following example illustrates this. A middle-aged vicar found he was losing interest in his work and felt it was deteriorating as a result. After some talk he dreamed he was in a potting-shed with the windows boarded up with school forms. He then produced a series of dreams in which he found suitcases full of scrap iron and had to dispose of all sorts of rubbish and eventually found himself back by the potting-shed. This time the whole shed was in ruins and he found he was out in the sunlight; then he said, 'Now I know I ought never to have been ordained.'

We discussed all the wrong motives that had led to his ordination, and then I was able to show him that though he had gone into the ministry for the wrong reasons, he could remain in it for the right ones and really begin to fulfil his vocation adequately. Since then he has been able to be of far

[1] i.e. emotional energy, with the satisfaction its healthy expenditure brings.

greater help to people in difficulties and will obviously go on to an increasing ministry instead of a decreasing one. But unless someone with a knowledge of psychopathology had been available to help him at the critical point, it would have been very easy either to have renounced his orders and sought some other work, or to have broken down so badly because he could not face this step that he might have been invalided out permanently to prevent him going on with it.

Some difficulties in married life at this age are similar in origin. The difficulties of life with the particular partner loom large because neither is really facing the necessary changes, and thoughts of previously discarded partners begin to emerge, hinting that if only they had been chosen, things would have been different. This can happen even where people are happily married. The urge to fulfil other aspects of the personality than the ones actually developed forces itself through at times and may even lead to unfaithfulness with someone who reminds the individual of one of his or her earlier attachments prior to the actual choice of the marriage partner. A deeper understanding of this enables clergy or others to help those in this position to realise they are falling into the most serious temptation of middle age— namely, regressing to something desirable in the past, instead of going forward *to make the best of the future*. If they can help both the one who has been unfaithful, and the partner who has been hurt by it, to understand this, repentance and real forgiveness may enable both partners to go forward creatively for the future—and separation or divorce may be prevented.

It may seem surprising to stress *regression to the past* as the most serious temptation of the middle aged. But in the light of what has been said about the possibility of life after middle age becoming spiritually deeper, and making its contribution to culture, it can be seen to be so. The critical point is here: Can we let go the things of the past, with their partial fulfil-

ments, realising the deficiences only too obvious, the opportunities we have failed to make the most of, and the smallness
of our real stature, can we let these go and concentrate on
adapting to the changes of a future that at first may seem full
of disillusionment, a perpetual frustration of our present
desires? Only those really able to look forward, not backwards
like Lot's wife, can find the increasing spiritual power of
middle age which can continue to deepen and make life ever
more worth living right on to old age. As was said in the
chapter on the problems of youth, if we can accept ourselves,
with all the deficiencies of our own youth *still leaving scars
on us*, and try to give young people opportunities we ourselves lacked, we may save our souls alive. If, on the other
hand, we seek to develop the youthful qualities we now find
we lack instead of those relevant to our age, we find we lose
the confidence and fellowship of both young and old—
'Mutton dressed up as lamb' is a common expression of this,
and the middle-aged philanderer is laying up for himself an
empty and unsatisfied old age.

There are other tendencies that create problems for the
middle aged; for example, if life has not been too successful,
there may be either a strong inclination to blame circumstances
and our environment, to get bitter and resentful about it or
to feel so depressed at our own inefficiency that we see only
our failures and get an *equally distorted view*. The extreme
form of the first way of evading our own responsibility is
seen in mental hospitals as 'paranoia'; a persecution complex
is only one stage further of this attempt to blame everything
but ourselves. The extreme form of the depression of middle
age is seen in such hospitals as melancholia; the melancholic,
however, blames everything in himself except the right thing,
his lack of courage in facing real problems. So paranoia or
depression alike loses contact with the *inner reality making for
sanity*, which is able to admit its own failures or sins squarely
and consequently becomes able to repent of them effectively

and thus outgrow them. This is not, of course, to ignore the physical aspect of psychosis. There is some real incapacity which, however, if it had been recognised and accepted earlier and adjustment to it made, might have prevented the deep melancholia which ignores all the positive assets or opportunities.

If regression is the most serious temptation of the middle aged, sublimation is its most serious task and opportunity. Instinctive energy must be harnessed to fulfil aims that are culturally, socially and personally acceptable. The primitive narcissism of the young child or immature adolescent must be completely outgrown. Objective fluctuations of youthful taste, the acquisitiveness of the scalp-hunter, whether the scalps be stamps, moths, butterflies or 'loves', must be sublimated into the respect for property compatible with its cultural and social value. To accumulate a library of well-read books is a sublimation of acquisitiveness that is socially useful. To buy up a collection of books beyond our capacity to appreciate in order to display a furnished library is an adolescent perversion of it.

One problem I would suggest as pre-eminently one for the middle aged is re-thinking and re-orienting our ideas about property. It was pointed out in the chapter on youth that there seemed to be a clash between the ideas of the pre-adolescent about property and our own complicated one. We see that greed and possessiveness is at the root of many troubles international and social. The Church paradoxically ow immense wealth which is in the hands of the Ecclesiast Commissioners, and is always struggling to make ends mee The Franciscan idea of the holiness of 'poverty' might be necessary at that time as a challenge to the self-indulgence of the rich. But extreme poverty is as inimical to the full development of the life of the spirit as preoccupation with vast riches can be. Moreover, personality does develop with the responsibility of 'property'. The child who learns to take care of limited but sufficient number of toys gains in the sense of responsibility. The adolescent who is given an allowance to make do for clothes as well as amusements grows more capable through so doing. The young married couple learning to stretch an income to cover the expenses of a home, saving up for furniture to improve it, are much more mature than those living in furnished lodgings.

So it is not the *fact* of property that is the trouble. It is our *attitude* to it. Possessions may help us to grow mature, possessiveness roots us in ourselves and re-inforces the primitive narcissism which must be outgrown if the spiritual life is to progress to full maturity.

Spiritual maturity does not coincide with physical maturity. It lies ahead, and thus there is still a *goal* in front of the middle aged who have passed the height of their physical reproductive powers, and in going on towards this further goal, life becomes *more* and not less worth living.

An interesting confirmation of the idea expressed in this recognition of a third stage in human development which can lead to a fuller life up to old age is given by Dr. Martin Gumpert. He had interviewed many notable old people who were still living and working happily in their eighties. He found they all seemed to enjoy their lives far beyond the average middle-aged individual. They had all unceasingly used their intelligence and continued to learn and grow.

Dr. Gumpert suggested that old age can develop a creative urge and a power of its own and that life as a whole may become richer and happier when we start to discover the treasures of old age now hidden under old age's miseries.

The time to prepare for this full flowering and completion of the life-cycle, instead of its frustration and decay, is during middle age. Once the position is realised and the *intention* of going forward has been made, progress can begin. Jung points out that the process of 'individuation' as he calls it, the development of the whole personality, conscious and unconscious together, demands its initiation by an *act of will*, a real intention and determination. One does not *drift* into maturity. So, when expressed in religious terms, the maturing of the prayer life, the deepening of our communion with God from middle age onwards demands a *deliberate* and conscious surrender to the indwelling of the Holy Spirit. It has frequently been pointed out that the higher levels of Christian experience are rarely reached today for lack of adequately trained spiritual directors. Jung too emphasises the need for guidance through the pitfalls that accompany individuation.

The need for prayer, so deep rooted in the human heart, is shown by the wide range of religious forms and ceremonies from the primitive savage with his totem, altar circles such as Stonehenge, to vast cathedrals and the wonderful range of sacred music. Man has put his best energies into this, and today the need is to deepen our response to God and discover the forms of religious experience appropriate to our own stage of development in an industrial and scientific age.

CHAPTER VI

Fallen Angel or Risen Ape?

MEN'S hearts in these days are so often failing them for fear: what is wrong with a world with such unprecedented control over the material world, wherein the youngest school-child can, by the turn of a switch, flood a room with light or the glories of a symphony concert, and yet men are also striving to perfect ever more powerful weapons of destruction? What is wrong with us? Are we fallen angels or risen apes?

The query indicates the paradox of our position with hopes and aspirations far beyond the range of apes, yet with a bodily structure closely akin to them and physical needs for food, which has to be obtained from without through our own efforts just as that of animals has to be sought by them.

Philosophers have tried to answer the question in many ways. Some have accepted the idea of a fall of man, the fallen angel idea. On that view man once *was* perfect, but through sin lost his heritage and now gropes his way back to the realm whence 'trailing clouds of glory' he came, through all the painful consequences of his original sin. On the other hand, actual historical evidence in fossil remains of the evolution of higher, more complex forms from simpler ones, supports the idea of man as rising from more primitive levels. The presence of vestigial organs in our own bodies, the appendix and the Eustachian tubes which are remnants of the gill slits of fishes, for example, indicate a long pre-human history, which has its effect upon our actual constitution, mentally as well as physically.

In the early years of this century the 'Risen Ape' idea was in the ascendant. Man had grown so far from his primitive beginnings and there was thought to be an era of continuous

progress ahead. Dachau and Belsen in the heart of Christen-
dom, followed by Hiroshima, have shaken the idea of continuous progress and have seemed to show that man can very
easily revert to the 'ape and the tiger' within.

But is this true? The ape and the tiger kill to live; they kill
for food, and when satisfied they don't go on killing. There
is more in the evil in the heart of man than the relics of ape
and tiger—or donkey! Man can *intend* to kill, maim and torture his fellow men for the sake of an idea, and other men can
accept the agonies inflicted *voluntarily* rather than conform. A
Christ, a Socrates, and a host of martyrs throughout the ages,
including many in concentration camps in recent years, show
there *is* something in man that he values more than sheer
physical life, something worth dying for, and therefore something worth living for.

Moreover, surely in the *perversion* of this in the Inquisitor,
the torturer and the brutalities of those who argue that the
end justifies the means there is also a glimpse of that something more than animal that has given rise to the idea of man
as a *fallen* being, a fallen angel.

Yet man is unique, neither angel nor ape. Capable of rising
to great heights of selflessness, of devotion, of creativity, yet
man is also capable of falling into depths of evil that no animal
could achieve. It is this paradox that gives rise to the antithesis
of Fallen Angel or Risen Ape.

But if instead of trying to off-shoulder our responsibility
onto any other kind of being, angelic or animal, we try to
accept ourselves as we *are*, functioning uniquely in relation to
a wide variety of environment, we may solve the paradox in
life that defeats us conceptually. We function physically in
interaction with the whole material aspect of the universe,
containing and utilising atoms of various kinds in particular
combinations that enable us to transform our food into our
own bodies, as well as the impact of rays from the sun,
oxygen from the air and moisture from rain. This involves

a whole cosmical interrelatedness. We are distinguishable forms of life, but not separable from the whole complex web of life, with bacteria, helpful and harmful, and an instinctive life which we share with the animal world, without which we would be unable to survive on earth.

Yet this is not the whole story. We also function emotionally in relation both to our own natures and to other people, and to ideas only held in imagination. We interact socially on our own level of culture, whether savage or civilised, with a respect for social solidarity, so that solitary confinement is one of the worst forms of punishment. We interact intellectually with the thinkers of all ages, races and climes through books, paintings, architecture and the relics left behind by other cultures for our interpretation. We interact spiritually with each other as we rise to personal relationships which include a measure of self-commitment to the fellowship, whether between marriage partners, friends, a team of workers each contributing to the skill of the whole, and ultimately in response to the creative Mind expressed in and through all that is.

The range of our personal development increases with the range of the environment to which we respond and within which we function with an ever-deepening measure of responsibility and insight.

Here within the heart of man we find, cheek by jowl, a mixture of saint and sinner, wise man and fool. The most holy have their weak spots, their blind spots and their black spots. The most depraved have their gleams of goodness, something to which it is possible to appeal if we can reach it without the recoil from the evil that breaks the rapport with the good.

One way of looking at man that may combine an element from the conception of the fallen angel idea and that of the risen ape is the realisation of a collective as well as an individual aspect of personality. Jung's conception of the collective or racial unconscious as the matrix out of which the personal unconscious and finally the fully personal individual develops gives us a hint. An analysis of dreams shows recurrent themes akin to primitive myths that seem to indicate a primitive substratum that can be tapped by appropriate means.

Within this substratum, primordial images—archetypes as Jung calls them—symbolise gods and devils, angels and satyrs, a whole primitive mythology. The emergence of these supra-personal images into consciousness brings with them a sense of the numinous and the uncanny, and the ego feels itself in an alien world and that in some way it is estranged from its high estate in that collective and supra-personal mode of mental functioning. Man feels guilty, and his very guilt provokes a reaction from still deeper levels of the unconscious. As he wrestles with the demons of the underworld and his own guilt, the protective redemptive elements wrought out in the very fibres of the being of mankind through the *actual* love and self-sacrifice that has been achieved in the lives of countless individuals brings a sense of forgiveness. He may have fallen far from his high estate, but someone or something greater than himself has reached down to him and reconciled him to a reality that is beyond him.

Here skill is needed, lest the very 'mana'[1] won from the depths swells the ego and a real inflation of personality follows, instead of the maturely integrated individual who has come to terms with the hidden good and evil within himself, without identifying himself with either.

The process of 'individuation', as Jung calls it, the making whole of the personality, depends upon the ability of the conscious personality to differentiate and integrate all that is within, to include the 'shadow side' we all tend to disown and so leave it free to wreak its evils unchecked until the results

[1] Mana may be translated as 'super-normal power'—either good or bad, beyond that of every-day experience. For sanity it is essential to keep one's 'psychical distance' from it and not identify oneself with it.

become so disastrous that we are compelled to take stock again.

Each man has to win his manhood through this fundamental conflict. The cumulative effects of the actual triumph of love and co-operation over hate and destruction which is involved in the actual survival cf man as a species make each individual feel guilty at falling short as he finds also within *himself* the cumulative effects of the failure of countless individuals to win through to their own maturity.

A guilty conscience is not just inspired by Christianity. It is a common fact of human experience. Christianity shows one way of overcoming it, with its stress on the fundamental nature of God as love, and a love that can redeem the sinner. But much Christianity capitulated to the fear from which Christ came to set us free, and fear of hell became more potent than the love of God. Where fear reigns, repression follows and the real nature cannot function in harmony. Hiroshima is a tragic witness to this. Only a love great enough to accept the whole self as it is, with its mingled good and evil instead of a narrowly 'respectable' self, can make us *whole* and set us free for the life more abundant that overflows from those who have faced their worst and found the deeper springs of life welling up from within.

Koestler suggested the central focal point of personality should be at the junction of Yogi and Kommissar, not splitting into one or the other, but balancing elements from both.

Dreams during analysis often indicate this blending of opposites into something more durable than either in conflict. One showed a pair of scales with gold coins on one side and iron counters on the other. The scales then broke with the weight and the gold and iron coins mingled. A flame shot up and melted them and the alloy that resulted looked rather like bronze, and was harder and more useful than gold, and more beautiful than iron and was also rust free. Out of the alloy a small boat was constructed that rode buoyantly on the sea of life.

Another dreamer, this time a woman, saw one woman about her own age dressed in white and another in black. They talked together for a time and then she found that one was wearing a white blouse with a black skirt and the other a black blouse with a white skirt. Each had accepted something from the other and yet each had kept something of its own characteristics. The personality was thus becoming better balanced, instead of an idealised self in white with the shadow self in black behind the scenes, as instinct and spirit began to function in harmony, neither fallen angel nor risen ape, but a woman in the making.

Perhaps a brief note may be helpful to readers not practically familiar with psychological analysis and the significance of dreams as indicating unsuspected aspects of our problems and attitudes. If we look on our minds as somewhat like icebergs with one-seventh above the surface and six-sevenths below it, the processes occurring below the surface can obviously greatly influence the direction in which the iceberg moves as a whole, and may even drive it in an opposite direction to that which one would expect from the winds above the surface, if a strong current is going the opposite way underneath.

As we probe into the human mind, we find that the study of dreams, of visions, of slips of the tongue, as well as of neurotic symptoms has opened up a new world for the understanding of life.

Once when lecturing to a group of clergy, one of them asked if I could explain why he had dreamed the night before that he couldn't find the service in the prayer book. On asking for more details, he said it was the marriage service he could not find. The bride and bridegroom were waiting and he was feverishly turning over the pages of the prayer book, but woke up without having found it.

On my asking him if there was any special reason why he did not want to marry the next couple on the register, he looked at me in amazement. 'Yes,' he said, 'an elderly widower had called the day before to ask me to put up the bans for himself and a nineteen-year-old girl, and I had thought this would be disastrous.' His reluctance to celebrate the wedding had expressed itself in his inability to find the service in the dream, but he had not seen the connection for himself.

Slips of the tongue, too, reveal a deeper motivation. A very well-known one was the report of a 'bottle-scarred' war veteran, which was then corrected into a 'battle-scared' one. The unconscious depreciation in both versions triumphed over the consciously intended praise in a 'battle-scarred veteran'.

Neurotic symptoms also reveal a purposiveness and relevance, however contrary to the conscious aims of the person concerned. The headache that gives a 'reasonable excuse' for not going to some function we don't want to attend, is very common. It is easy to rationalise and say to ourselves, 'I would go if I didn't feel so rotten', instead of having the moral courage to admit to ourselves that we don't *want* to go then deciding deliberately whether to go or to cut it, which would have avoided the headache and maintained integrity.

This must not, of course, be taken to mean that all headaches are neurotic evasions of some conflict between desire and duty. But if anyone subject to headaches checks up on how often they occur so as to prevent him doing something difficult or unpleasant, and how often they interfere with hobbies and enjoyments he may suspect a psychological basis if they all come under the first heading, and a physical one if they occur indiscriminately under both.

Hysterical blindness is a simple example of becoming unable to register seeing anything to avoid seeing something specific. One man became completely blind to words, unable to read anything, and it was discovered during analysis that it was to avoid seeing the names of those killed in battle. He could not just go blind to them, but went blind to all words. Here one would suspect a deeper motivation, and that there was some unconscious guilt associated with the list of casualties. Had he shirked joining up and running the risk himself?

Psychological analysis is designed to help us to become aware of the deeper levels of mental functioning, so that instead of wasting a lot of energy in a conflict which is insoluble so long as one aspect of it is unknown to us, there can be a greater harmony between the conscious and unconscious aspects of personality, as was illustrated in the two dreams quoted in which there was a blending of black and white, of gold and iron, to reach a serviceable equilibrium in which both sides were respected as equally valid. The unconscious is not merely evil, it is also the matrix out of which that which is good emerges, and we cannot draw on the deeper resources for creative living if we disown the residue of the effects of the evil in our own personal lives or those of the race which are also within us. The mythologies in which the hero has to overcome some great evil or go through severe tests before he can reach his goal symbolise the reality of the struggle to harmonise the conflicting elements within us.

In *Essays on Religion, Life and Psychotherapy*, which is in course of preparation, an account is given of the part that may be played by psychological analysis, not just for the cure of neurotics, but for the maturing of the healthy minded, and both analysis and spiritual direction can be used as *aids* to the developing of the spiritual life.

In the next chapter we see how psychology can help us to enrich our prayer life and deepen our communion with God.

CHAPTER VII

Psychology and Prayer

THERE are many possible ways of treating such a subject as psychology and prayer. The method followed here is intended for those who believe in God and who all in varying ways pray to Him. The aim is to consider prayer in the light of the discoveries psychology has made of the ways our minds work, in order that we may learn to pray more effectively, with less wastage of energy. It is practical rather than theoretical for the reader of average intelligence who desires to profit by the results of modern research and who is sure enough of God to realise that *all* truth comes from Him.

The part played by suggestion in meditation, by desire in petition, by imagination in bringing our wills into harmony with God, and by faith in effective intercession will be considered. Together with this, the psychological basis for penitence and the need for disciplined growth through moral effort is indicated. This leads on to the nature of worship and the goal of prayer, based on Our Lord's example, as growing communion with 'Our Father'.

Prayer

True prayer should fulfil the principles Christ formulated when He said, 'Ask and it shall be given to you' (petition); 'seek and ye shall find' (search); 'knock and it shall be opened unto you' (the great adventure of contemplation, wherein the unsearchable riches of Christ which are unreeled before us bow our heads in spontaneous adoration, quickening our wills as a result).

The pre-supposition of communion is *likeness of outlook, spiritual sympathy, and moral unity of purpose*. If prayer is to be a real communion with God, then it is only possible if God be self-revealing.

There are many people we meet whom we feel it would be a privilege to know better, yet the more we come into contact with them, the more we realise will be for ever beyond our understanding unless they choose to let us into their inmost hearts, whence spring the fruits in action that make us feel we are in the presence of those who are far beyond us. We can see what they do, but how they do it only they can tell.

So with God. We see much of what He does in the world around—and science daily adds to the wonder of His works, pointing to a Being far greater than our ancestors could ever have realised as their source. If we have a glimmer of imagination in us, we are led to wonder about the nature of such a Being—and as we ponder something of awe falls upon us, almost the invisible God breaks in upon us. We begin dimly to realise His presence—something—someone, other than ourselves, in whose presence we are overwhelmed at our own littleness, yet strangely unafraid. Otto has shown throughout all religious experience this peculiar blend of emotion in the presence of the *felt* unseen which he calls 'numinous'—the Holy—'*Mysterium tremendum, mysterium fascinans*'—awe-inspiring, fascinating. 'Take of thy shoes from off thy feet, for the ground whereon thou standest is holy ground.'

Otto shows it rises from a grisly demonic dread to the highest flights of mystical ecstasy as a strangely compelling experience in which the believer cannot doubt he is in the presence of a greater Being than himself, whom he can but worship.

Yet at first his religion is as primitive as his science. He cannot help praying, cannot help trying to get into some sort of relationship with the unseen world he feels is real, but he knows not how to pray as he ought, because he knows not God as He is. So, long before Christ came to show us the

Father, men looked for one who should come from heaven to throw light upon their darkness. The need of every race was a deliverer—a saviour—however crudely postulated, God was preparing men for His own fuller revelation of Himself, and through those who responded most fully, as the prophets in the Old Testament, He led others to expect a yet fuller revelation, until in the fullness of time Christ came that we might know God as He is. That we might understand at last, He lived as man, teaching us in our own language through all the varied experiences of life, to find God *everywhere*. As man, Christ too reached out in prayer, communing in spirit with the Father, growing into likeness of outlook and spiritual sympathy through their moral unity of purpose. Seeing Him pray, His disciples could not doubt that He had found what they sought—fellowship with God. So they said 'Lord, Master, teach us to pray.' Let us join with them, for if prayer is communion, then only God can teach it— and for that He became incarnate.

He began as all true prayer begins—with God—saying, 'Our Father'. Gone was the terrible Moloch demanding sacrifice, and gone was the stern implacable judge; gone was the unknowable dreaded God, whose wrath must be appeased at any cost: gone was the whole pantheon of gods and goddesses, and in their place He taught us 'Our Father'. Someone we can trust and in some measure understand. Far beyond us, yes, but in the closest relationship to us. And as we say 'Our Father' the realisation of the untold millions to whom He is Father bows our heads with deeper awe than all the majesty of the power behind the Universe can evoke, as we realise the limitless nature of such love. So contemplating such a God 'Who is in heaven', the natural response of man is 'Hallowed be Thy name'. The pattern prayer is based on sound psychology, as would be expected from Christ.

Then swiftly such a vision of God, firing our imagination, leads us to pray, 'Thy kingdom come', and stirs our wills to strive joyfully. 'Thy will be done, on earth as it is in heaven.'

From this desire springs the natural realisation of the need for power from on high to fulfil it. It is not our own kingdom or will we seek to see triumphant on earth, as in heaven, but Our Father's—and only He can bring that.

So begins the third stage, concerned with our equipment for life in the kingdom of God on earth. 'Give *us* this day our daily bread'—food for body, mind and spirit—for Christ showed men could not live by bread alone, but by every word proceeding forth from God. It is a prayer for all things needful for life on earth day by day. The emphasis on 'daily', illustrates Christ's realisation of the deepest needs of our nature, which is so prone to worry about tomorrow, instead of preparing for it today.

Then as our faith is quickened thus in the realisation that Our Father will provide, will make our wants His care as we go about His business—the clause *follows* the dedication of our wills—we become aware of the moral demand and our failure to fulfil it. The Holy becomes ethical, righteous, not merely numinous, evoking penitence as well as awe—and with true penitence, love for others, the fulfilment of the law. 'Forgive us our trespasses, as we forgive them that trespass against us.' 'Father forgive them, they know not what they do.' We who live after Christ's passion, know how royally He fulfilled it in action. While we were yet dead in sins Christ died for us—that henceforth He might call us friends. But friendship, communion as we have seen, demands a spiritual sympathy, and a moral unity of purpose, so we find the need for our own forgiveness ere we have the power to forgive our enemies. He who is without sin will not seek to cast a stone at another. Fear of particular sins in ourselves is often the cause of violent antagonism towards others who have fallen into it. The moral condition of *full* fellowship in the kingdom is freedom from our own complexes, which bias our own judgment and issue in an unforgiving spirit that widens the breach in fellowship wrought by sin, instead of the forgiving spirit that leaps out to bridge it at any cost.

So, from this, those who have prayed so far as Christ has bidden them have learned the power of temptation and their own weakness. Only the man or woman who knows his weakness is strong. St. Peter with all his impulsive lovableness could yet fail his Master in His hour of crisis—and Jesus, knowing him better than he knew himself, knew he would fail then. But he also knew that the realisation of his weakness would lead him to be willing to receive from Christ the strength he thought he had in himself and now found was lacking. On the rock of the *humility and faith* that sprang from that, Christ said His church should rest.

So, recognising this, we pray like Christ, 'If it be possible let this cup pass. Lead us not into temptation, but deliver us from evil,' and in the 'tough humility that springs from an active dependence' we can with thankful faith exultingly conclude. 'For Thine is the kingdom, the power and the glory, for ever and ever—' ending, as we began, with God.

Throughout this prayer there is a swift interplay between God and man. The response to each clause evokes the next naturally. God as well as man plays His part in evoking the triumphant 'deliver us from evil', in the faith that He not only can, but *will*. Prayer has been communion, has issued in a common purpose, a moral and spiritual sympathy, as we thus learn to discern the mind of God.

How is it then that so much of our prayer falls below this standard? Can psychology help us to use our minds more fruitfully, to fulfil our side of prayer better? Can it show us why we often fail? How can we link our ideals to our wills? They seem so far apart.

This problem has faced man in every religion, and there is no developed religion that has not tried to meet it. Meditation upon truths that are known is always a step towards the apprehension of truths yet beyond us. If truth is to be active in us, it must go deeper, must grip our imagination, and through that release the energy of our wills that were too feeble to act out what our conscience approved. *Faith is belief we translate into action.* Truth has no power on earth unless we can incarnate it within living beings, able to act upon it. Love is meaningless unless it issues in service.

There is no need here to describe the various methods of meditation evolved by different races or communities. It seems to me that it will be more helpful if we consider the common basis in the natural laws of our minds through which God works, which can then be adapted to individual needs or differences.

Suggestion and Meditation

The parable of the sower illustrates the use of suggestion in planting spiritual truths in our minds so that they spring up spontaneously, bringing forth fruit twenty-fold, thirty-fold, a hundred-fold. There is no attempt to reason about it, to convince people. The word of God is scattered abroad for all. The kind of suggestion to which we respond unconsciously depends upon the kind of person we are. If we belong to the group of people never so happy as when discussing all their ailments, we are more likely to succumb to, say, a 'flu germ' in the next epidemic than if we belonged to the group who believed disease had to be fought by every means in our power, and that God was with us in the fight. The germ would be the same, the suggestion that it was infectious and therefore we might catch it would be the same, but the ground on which the suggestion fell would be different, and so would be the result.

This principle is just as true with regard to ideas affecting our minds as our bodies. Before truth can come home to us as true, we must have a disposition towards truth enabling us to see it. Before beauty can be recognised as beauty we must have a capacity for apprehending it. So far as we know, the dog, looking at a view that makes us gasp for sheer loveliness, is more interested in the smells, and the possibility of an exciting chase in following them up.

So, too, before we can respond to love, we must have the capacity to love in us, or we either feed on it as parasites, or sweep it aside as weak sentimentality, not worthy of strong men who worship power, saying the weak must go to the wall, they are stopping progress.

So we see in suggestion both the nature of the seed-thought sown, and the nature of the ground in which it is sown matter, if it is to be translated into action. Not only can we not gather grapes off thorns, but even if we plant a vine it may not be able to grow for lack of proper nourishment from the soil.

Now suppose we have found some things really worth thinking about, worth pondering on—glimpses of truth and beauty which make us long to share in them, heroic acts, wonderful devotion to truth, to art, to God or to home and country. Yet the harder we think about them the more impossible it seems to get such impulses, such life, to take root in ourselves. Suppose the first effect of something winning our admiration is its utter contrast with ourselves as we are, making us dissatisfied with ourselves as we have never been before. What are we to do? The harder we try to 'go and do likewise', the more unlike our pattern we seem to ourselves to become. What is wrong with our method? We have no doubt about the quality of the seed. We see clearly enough for that, but the ground seems strangely inhospitable to it. As Christ said, it may be too stony. We may be too wrapped in our own concerns even to try to give root to the vision which caught our attention for the moment. It may be clothed with weeds, unkept, untidy, uncared for, never having had the discipline of spade or hoe, which can make the best even of poor ground, by letting in fresh light and air. Though we long for the crop of beautiful flowers true to the seed sown, the weeds of careless habits, the tares of deliberate sin, the thistles of doubt we have never had the courage to face squarely, all get in the way and the word of God cannot find a resting place.

It may be shallow ground—the attention quickly caught by every new thing, never remaining long enough on any to bring forth fruit of its kind, either good or bad.

It may be swept away quickly by a suggestion opposite in kind—the birds of the air carry it away, or it may fall in good ground—a trained and disciplined mind, and so bring forth fruit in varying measure. What can we do about it? We know more than enough truth by which to live, if we could only live by it. How can we improve the soil of our hearts and minds, how can we prepare for good seed that it may grow? How, if there is fruit twenty-fold, can we bring it up to a hundred-fold?

Let us consider the part played by suggestion in meditation. In a previous book [1] it was shown that suggestion should be subdivided in various ways. It is a natural process of the human mind and imagination through its use can stir our wills, can help us to translate our ideas into action, voluntary or involuntary. Suggestion is a good servant but a bad master. Can we call it in here to help our meditations to become fruitful? Can science throw light upon the way the geniuses of every religion have met this need by meditation? Let us see. Suggestion is defined by McDougall as the acceptance with conviction of a communicated proposition in the absence of logically adequate grounds for its acceptance.[2] This issues in appropriate thought, feeling or action spontaneously. The nature of the ideas that will germinate so depends upon the kind of mind on to which they fall. It is difficult to plant an evil suggestion in the mind of a good man. Fortunately, it is

---

[1] A. G. Ikin, *Religion and Psychotherapy*.
[2] W. McDougall, *Social Psychology*, p. 97.

easier to help a bad man to become better by leading him to dwell on better things.

Suggestion may be spontaneous or deliberate. If a chance word falls on a responsive mind it will take root. It may suddenly go home and become operative, quite apart from our wills. For example, someone may say that riding with your back to the engine will make you sick and a sensitive child may respond and be sick under those conditions for years. On other children it might have no effect. Yet they too in later years might struggle vainly against fears due to other suggestions which had had their effect, such as fear of the dark, due to having been frightened with tales of the bogy man, or his equivalent. So too it is with suggestions we would welcome. We all know this. No one has put out effort, a word is spoken, yet somehow it becomes alive with power and we are never quite the same afterwards. Or we see someone doing things we have done unthinkingly before in a new light and are horrified. Never again can we do that without the twinge of conscience then awakened making us uneasy. We have got to change ourselves somehow as a result.

Spontaneous suggestion is one of God's most welcome gifts. If all our growth had to depend upon our deliberate efforts to foster it, it would be a poor stunted thing. The seed that germinates spontaneously prepares the way for that which needs to be fostered deliberately. If, therefore, we want good seed to grow spontaneously, we should bring our children into the atmosphere in which it is natural, and as we grow older, we should seek the books and friends whose influence shall prepare the ground in which 'whatsoever things are lovely' may take root. Most of us owe more to our friends than we shall ever realise. The suggestions with love behind them take root most deeply. Our deepest influence is not due to what we say or do, but to what we are.

If suggestions of which we disapprove have taken root, experience shows that the effort to root them out by will only fixes them more deeply. This illustrates the Law of Reversed Effort. But what suggestion has caused, suggestion can cure. This is at the basis of the practice of trying to overcome some sin by meditation upon the corresponding virtue. I am never quite sure personally whether the cure in that case is not worse than the disease. It can induce such a self-conscious virtue that it is worse than the recognised sin. I believe that to be effective we must meditate upon a person— Christ, or someone we love—as they go about their work thinking of them in action and letting that influence soak in indirectly. Otherwise we tend to pray for humility as if it could be bought by the yard, or gentleness weighed out by the pound. No amount of thinking about humility will give it to us, *it is in mutual service it grows*. No self-culture, however arduous, can give it. I do not advise suggestion as a means to developing individual virtues. It is not at all certain whether individual virtues exist. There may be virtuous individuals, great souls whom to know is to love and be educated thereby. But if so they never grew by self-culture. True self-development is always the by-product of self-forgetful service.

It must not be forgotten, however, that it is necessary to *accept* one's self before one can effectively forget one's self. Otherwise the repressed ego vitiates and sterilises our best endeavours to serve. Many Christians fail through not realising this. Manuals of devotion which aim at repressing the self instead of expressing it have been responsible for much of the waste of effort that is so depressing in the history of religion.

Nevertheless there is a part to be played by suggestion in helping meditation to be a real tiller of the soil of human minds, a real watering of the seeds we long to embody in ourselves or in the world, a real help towards growing fellowship with God.

Just as we can learn how to train our imagination and

educate our wills in the service of health, so can we learn how
to develop them in a growing communion with God through
which little by little we become like Him, as we begin to see
Him as He is. For this meditation upon Him and upon His
works is essential. It is in a large part through meditation that
the Spirit of Truth who is with us becomes operative *in* us;
that the Spirit of Beauty awakens in us the need for harmony
everywhere; that the Spirit of Love, which is the love of
Christ constraining us to joyful service, can become incarnate,
bringing the kingdom of love on earth as in heaven.

Christ said, 'As a man thinketh in his heart, so he is.' He
showed that not only the lustful act, but the lustful thought,
was sin. He showed that murder and anger differ only in
degree, and that of the two, anger may be the more deadly,
hurting a sensitive soul, whereas murder only touches the
body. Everywhere we see Christ placing the emphasis on the
inward disposition, knowing if that be right then outward
acts would express it naturally. The study of suggestion shows
that ideas with an emotional accompaniment, fear or desire,
tend to issue in action independently of our wills. I think that
is what Christ meant by 'thinketh in his heart'.

We are quite able to walk on a plank on the ground, but
spread it across a chasm or between the towers of a cathedral
and fear of falling in most of us would issue in a fall. This
is very significant morally. Fear of sin keeps the mind so
focussed upon itself and its weakness that when concrete
temptation comes, as it comes to all, our wills are paralysed
by fear and we find that we have literally 'fallen into sin',
which is quite different from a deliberate *act* of sin. A great
deal of the trouble sincere Christians have with themselves is
due to confusing 'falling into sin' and 'sinning'. Both are sin,
both break the law of love and fellowship with God or man.
We are responsible for both. It is not a question of weakly
shelving our responsibility onto our subconscious mind. It is
our mind. But the prevention of sin must follow different

lines according to whether the sin is in spite of our wills or through our wills. In this chapter it is hoped to show that meditation is one of the most effective preventers of 'falling into sin'. In the next one, penitence and the need for moral effort in overcoming sins of the will, will be considered.

Meditation and suggestion are concerned with sins or diseases of the *imagination*, which are much the most difficult to cure and which cause more trouble in the world than does deliberate sin, as well as often driving sincere Christians to the verge of despair. Someone was asked whether he would rather have the burden of deliberate sin or 'original sin' removed. Unhesitatingly he said the latter. And I believe that what has been called 'original sin' is just the kind of disorder in our minds that leads us to 'fall into sin' as described above. If so, then St. Paul's prescription to think upon everything lovely and of good report is a very sound one for replacing the 'mind of sin' with the 'mind of Christ' and so delivering us from 'the body of this death'.

Just as a sewage pumped into the sea is rendered harmless by the action of air and bacteria made possible by its dilution in the vast volume of water, so when we open our minds deliberately to the purifying action of the love of God, dwelling on truth and beauty, our petty self-centredness is gradually replaced by a breadth of view that springs directly from that bracing contact with a mind or minds purer and richer than our own. Every book we read leaves us different, for good or ill. We have shared another's thoughts, and if the thoughts were worth sharing we are strengthened by them. If the thoughts were base ones and yet have attracted us, we are the worse. It may, of course, be necessary to read books that deal with bad and morbid subjects. Doctors, nurses, clergy and lawyers, for example, have to do so in the ordinary course of their work. But let us beware when we do so lest we find ourselves unconsciously being attracted by the evil we are seeking to be armed to cure. That which at first disgusts us can begin to interest us and colour our outlook and insidiously prepares the way for a lapse on our own part. The falls of some of those directly concerned with the prevention and cure of sexual misconduct are to be accounted for thus. So, too, are flagrant lapses on the part of temperance reformers. It is never easy to be in contact with any particular form of evil without either condemning it with the vindictiveness that implies a subconscious attraction to it or sooner or later falling a victim to its appeal. Here knowledge of the dangers and awareness of our own vulnerability are essential if we are to overcome evil with good and not be overcome by it. Self-righteousness is the prelude to an inevitable failure to eliminate the evil, issuing in intolerance of the actual evil fought.

In all this, suggestion plays its part for good or ill. We cannot eliminate it, we can only learn to use it aright. In meditation we deliberately seek to employ it to make our minds more receptive to truth, or beauty or love, by dwelling on thoughts that can inspire us and can lift us above our petty concerns into a wider, more spacious environment, wherein the truth shall make us free. It is very necessary to use it deliberately thus if our work leads us to deal with the baser side of human nature and counteract the suggestive influence of the morbid conditions with which we have to deal.

Meditation does not only mean thinking upon Biblical texts or passages. As has been mentioned earlier Tennyson could meditate upon the 'flower in the crannied wall' and know that if he knew all about it he would know God as He is. *Every work of God can lead us to God*, and we do well to start from the level of experience that arouses our interest spontaneously. If our desire is sincere, we need not fear that we shall stay in the outer courts and not find God because we do not start with Him. Christ bids us meditate on the lilies of the field if we would know the glory of God. Only when our imagination has been quickened thus can we rightly go on to God Himself. To start with God Himself for most of us ends in losing Him. In strain and effort to keep our minds from wandering we arise tired, unrefreshed, and feel inclined to say that meditation is obviously not for us, it must be the privilege—or the burden—of a few select souls. Whereas it is not meditation that is beyond us, we need it as we need light and air and food, but it is our method that is wrong.

We all know how difficult it is to remember a name we have forgotten, and how it seems to get further out of reach the harder we try to recall it; and how it just slips into our mind later on when we are no longer thinking about it. So with meditation; the harder we try to keep our minds on God, the further away from reality He will seem to be. The human mind cannot keep itself focussed on God; only God can draw it to Himself, so that is His business, not ours. Nevertheless, if we do want to know Him, let us begin with something that has happened and let our thoughts play *freely*, not determinedly, about that. It does not matter whether we start with a Gospel story—Jesus blessing little children, for example—or with some particular happening we have seen that gripped our attention and *won our admiration*. It does matter that we start contemplating *action*, not pious aspirations out of relation to life.

Freud has shown us how a single wish or intention can inspire and hold together a great diversity of thought leading up to the fulfilment of the wish or intention, creating the solution as it goes. He calls it 'free association' as opposed to 'directed thinking'. Meditation makes use of this faculty of our minds. It is a work of art, not of logic, which is why we need to learn how to 'think creatively' as well as scientifically, if we are to worship God with *all* our minds, our hearts, our souls and our strength.

So, because in meditation we hope to draw nearer to the mind of God, that 'wish' or 'intention' will colour all our thinking. If only we let our minds play freely, not pulling them up sharply because they seem to have wandered from the point, we will find our thoughts become deeper and richer, and finally almost seem to be thinking themselves, to be breathed into us. The Spirit of Truth that is with us becomes alive in us, taking us into the Presence of God. That is the way in which meditation leads naturally on to contemplation, and that 'natural' contemplation is within the reach of *all* who seek God in prayer. Its form will differ with different temperaments. God speaks to each in language each can understand, which is why it is so important to start with our own language if we would learn His and not with that of someone else. The higher contemplation wherein the initiative seems to come from God is merely a continuation of this which defines a particular soul's channel of service. It is a vocational call, no higher than any other, but quite a definite one needed for the welfare of mankind. No straining or effort can produce it, only God can give it. So that is not our present concern.

The real gripping of our imagination by the Spirit of God, which is the *goal* of meditation, evokes in us an awareness of the contrast between God and ourselves. This involves penitence mingled with joy, which stimulates our wills to bridge it, to strive to follow at any cost. There is no true penitence without joy. Shame, remorse and hurt pride all play their part in what we often call penitence, but they are in the realm of feeling only. True penitence is rooted in the will and joy is an inevitable accompaniment, only blocked by the admixture of hurt pride that so often mars it.

Penitence and Moral Effort

We saw how the goal of meditation, the real gripping of our imagination by the Spirit of God, leads spontaneously to a recognition of the contrast with His perfect holiness. Isaiah's response is typical: 'I am a man of unclean lips.'

So also is that of St. Peter: 'Depart from me O Lord, for I am a sinful man.' Yet the very recognition of this shows our real affinity with the holiness that abases us. While we are 'dead in sins', we are not aware of the contrast—though our neighbours may be. We have lost our birthright of discerning good and evil, by choosing evil which increasingly blinds us to any alternative. The completely evil man could not be conscience stricken, nor could the completely good. To be conscience stricken is therefore *to be good enough to become aware of evil as evil*, through contrast with a good beyond us, yet akin, shaming us out of our self-righteous self-satisfaction, stinging us awake to possibilities previously unsuspected. In the realised Presence of God we begin dimly to know ourselves as we are. As our knowledge of God grows, so does our knowledge of ourselves and our fellow men. This is why the saints have always been more alive and sensitive to evil and imperfection than those who are less in touch with God.

There has been much confused thinking about sin in all religions. Yet all of them have realised it as not merely immoral, not merely anti-social, not only affecting our social relationships, but in some way connected with God. Sin is a specifically religious concept. It implies something deliberate, wilful, something evil that need not have been, something different from 'falling into sin' or into temptation through unsuspected weakness. Sin implies moral responsibility, that we could have acted otherwise and nothing but ourselves prevented us from having done so. Sin is always destructive of value. If penitence involves the reversal of this, then we can see that true penitence must be creative of that which sin destroys. If sin cuts us off from fellowship with God or man through its breaking the moral unity of purpose and sympathy of outlook necessary for communion, then penitence must restore that relationship. It must bring us back into that community of effort implied in fellowship, and so must affect our wills and not merely our feelings.

Much of what goes by the name of penitence is a mixture of remorse and hurt pride, which is utterly self-centred. We loathe ourselves for becoming the kind of self we have made ourselves, but it is because it is *we* who are in the wrong we bemoan it, not because the wrong is something alien to God and the universe, to be cast out at any cost to us. In true penitence, while feeling genuinely ashamed of having identified ourselves with evil, with having made it for the time being part of us, it is because it is evil, not because it is ourselves we are ashamed. Thus dissociating our sin from ourselves, and through penitence repudiating our past action or state, we reach out and strive to become better. True penitence strengthens our wills to fight against evil in any and every form in ourselves or in others. Self-pity and hurt pride, masquerading as penitence, instead of inspiring us to get up and do better next time, leave us helplessly bewailing our sinfulness in the hope that by sufficiently admitting the fact it will lead to some magical transformation that will alter us without effort, and without any desire to avoid the evil itself, only desiring to avoid its effect on us. False penitence is a wallowing in emotion, never touching our wills. We hope to appease an angry God by rolling in the dust before Him, and for the moment God is helpless. He can do nothing with someone who only cringes, there is no point of contact. His first command must be 'Son of man, stand upon thy feet.' *There must be self-respect before there can be true penitence.*

How His Father's heart must have ached at this awful misunderstanding of His nature that thought it did God honour by vilifying the creatures He had made, that thought to win favour by servility instead of service—what a pathetic caricature of God. Yet in the enormous over-emphasis on the sinfulness of man there was the truth that sin really mattered to God as well as to man. Only on Calvary could we realise just now much it mattered, when we saw God manifesting His love in action at such a cost in suffering to save us from our sin and from our misinterpretation of our sense of sin.

It is wounded love, crying in His death agony 'Father forgive them, they know not what they do', that makes the self-centredness of our early penitence fade away. When we see the effect of sin on the sinless, drawing from Christ Incarnate the cry 'My God, My God, why hast Thou forsaken Me?' there is no longer room for self-pity. A great horror at the nature of sin itself is aroused that strikes into the roots of our being, turning us resolutely from it, stirring our wills to fight it at any cost and evoking a great love for Him who gave Himself so royally.

The penitent thief illustrates this supremely. Dying in agony he realised was deserved, was the consequence of his own action, his own sinfulness, he saw one in like suffering who had not deserved it, who had gone about doing good. Instead of whining to be let off, saying that he had not known fully or that everybody did it, he showed his manhood in the simple acceptance of the fact that he had sinned, and in the Presence of the sinless was inspired to say, 'Lord, remember me when Thou comest into thy Kingdom.' Is it not amazing that the only bright gleam in that desperate darkness of Calvary came from a sinner who repented fearlessly, making no excuses, which enabled Christ to say 'This day shalt thou be with me in Paradise.' We shall never know how much that first fruit of His Passion on Calvary itself helped Christ to hold on in the hope of victory until He could say 'It is finished.' There, for ever pictured, we see the effect of Christ on sin. Sin died in the man who repented, and with Christ in Paradise there would be the communion and fellowship through that insight into and repudiation of evil which is true repentance. This would inevitably issue in a new birth unto righteousness.

Our deepest worship is evoked not by the culmination of beauty unspotted by evil but by the expression of Love shown forth on Calvary, wherefrom eternally the Risen Christ bears the marks of His passion, the indelible wounds of sin, engraved upon the very Being of the God who made us for Himself, whom we crucified ere we worshipped. Worship without penitence is a psychological impossibility in such a universe as ours. We can only worship with the very nature that has sinned. If we do not own our sin and turn from it, we have no power with which to worship.

Freud makes it very clear that repression prevents sublimation; that only the honest recognition of our sinful desires, together with the determination to find rightful channels for their activity, can issue in sublimation and form the basis of a stable personality. Worship that does not spring from penitence is a way of escape from Reality: a phantasy that lulls the moral self into a dangerous peace which is rudely broken when temptation arises and a consequent fall shatters our vision of so-called reality.

Some natures are more prone than others to mistake fervour of devotion divorced from action for real worship. They confuse *feeling* good with *being* good, and think their day's duty is done when they have taken the trouble to get up for an early service, after which they return to snap at their cook, who may have been up even earlier without the help of the service. They have never responded with the real worship that springs from some measure of communion with the Divine, not merely from one's own emotions, and which inevitably issues in actions that reveal the reality of that communion.

True worship, the love of one forgiven much, inspires moral endeavour, and, facing the foe, temptations can be overcome and their very driving power can reinforce our worship and our love, so that evil indeed has no more dominion over us.

This brings us to an important difference between sin and immaturity. A new birth unto righteousness is birth, not maturity. Once we have accepted freedom from sin through Christ, once we have turned resolutely from evil, to grow in fellowship with Him, we must not think we are full grown in righteousness and that we can sit down and leave it all to Christ. We must learn as babes how to live out the righteousness of Christ *under the conditions in which we are*. We must face temptation as He faced it. We must face even temptations from our past life, slack habits that only the formation of steady disciplined ones can counteract. We must start again at the very beginning, to learn how to live on earth the life triumphant over sin that He lived and calls us to share. Death unto sin does not mean freedom from temptation, it may even intensify it; *but it implies a refusal to consent to sin as necessary and the power to win through it*. The new birth unto righteousness quickens us to resist evil and enables us to overcome it with good. A new dynamic enters our lives and through conflict after conflict we grow in fellowship with Him who set us free, learning to discern as He did, learning to share the Mind of Christ as we face life in His Spirit.

As we grow, many things that were the best we could see or do previously have to be outgrown. There is temptation to cling to the good we know, to refuse to risk it on the next level on which we sometimes fear we may fail. But we rest in our progress at our peril. We have behind us and within us the whole power of Christ to make us like Himself, not to stop half way. To stop half way is to turn back from His way and lose the very power by which He had brought us so far. The moment we are satisfied our growth stops, and when growth stops decay begins to set in. Self-righteous self-satisfaction, resting in our own achievements instead of in God, cuts us off from the life of the spirit in which we have begun to glory as if it were our own right. The breaking down of our illusions and phantasies about ourselves and our own importance always involves a sense of utter insecurity, since that on which we have relied must be realised as a construct of our own minds and so dissolved by reality if our real selves, grounded in reality, are to function. The reality of the Divine, breaking through the illusions whereby our religion has been a way of escape from reality, seems to shatter us, leaving nothing of which we can be sure. It seems to knock the bottom not only out of our own ego but out of the world and even God Himself. Yet only through this turning-point, this utter emptiness and impotence, can contact with reality be achieved or maintained. While it is obvious that only in contact with reality can Reality function in and through us and so fulfil our real nature. At first growth, though real, is felt by us as failure, it is so alien to our primitive ambitions and phantasies; hence only as we lose our self-constructed lives can we begin to live out our real ones, not in an abstract Kingdom of Heaven, but in the real world wherein men live and love, suffer and sin, hope and despair, die and rise again. The message of psychotherapy reaffirms the Gospel demands. Demands which are strongly supported by the work of Karl Barth in his interpretation of the doctrine of St. Paul. Nothing less than re-birth and a new life can break through the bonds of illusion with which we have bound ourselves so securely, and which render us so impotent either to discern or fulfil the will of God. It is so much easier to fulfil our own desires and throw away our birthright as sons of God for a mess of pottage, that sooner or later will turn to dust and ashes, than to rise to our heritage, seeking the power of God to fulfil the will of God.

This illustrates the difference between 'Faith' and 'works' too. The effort to prepare by 'works', to run under one's own steam, quickly defeats itself, drawing on the ego instead of relying on the vital interaction between ego and environment which is the fruit of the faith that is contact with reality, and which springs from the humility (another measure of our contact with reality) that knows for the fulfiling of the will of God, God's power is essential: or in psychological language, that for efficiency in reality, reality is essential, not a self-limited and ego-centric effort, as if by our own efforts we could increase our stature.

Growth and 'works' *follow* faith. The feverish effort to prepare ourselves, setting almost unconsciously a standard out of relation to reality, quickly ends in exhaustion. The quiet trust, relying on the forces of spirit to bring about our preparation in time to enable us to meet the demands of the spirit, enables us to grow towards the standard of efficiency actually possible to us, instead of the phantastically high one we set ourselves. Then while seeming to ourselves to achieve less, we actually achieve more, because the 'works' that spring from the 'faith' that brings them into being are grounded in reality and thus are truly effective.

Once we have the power of the Love that has set us free, with us, we can like St. Paul rejoice in the Lord and learn how to turn everything to the furtherance of the Gospel. Every temptation can be turned into an opportunity *not* to sin, every difficulty can be turned into a challenge to overcome in Christ's own way. Like athletes who train that they may run without exhaustion, we should train ourselves daily to respond to the love of God, 'listening in' in prayer and meditation regularly that we may become attuned to Him everywhere and everywhen. Discipline inspired by love develops spiritual muscles, trained to wrestle against 'principalities and powers', trained to help others, to heal the sick, to cast out devils, to recover the fallen and bind up the broken-hearted, to bring the oil of joy for mourning. Freely we have received, freely we must give. And as we give we become able to receive more. This leads up to the fruits of communion in *effective* intercession.

Intercession

The part played by a faith in intercession must be considered next. Intercession is an overflow, the fruit of our communion with God. In the case of suggestion it has been shown that our *real conviction* decides the issue. But if intercession means anything, it is more than suggestion. Nevertheless, conviction does decide. Many of my readers will know the story of the woman who tried to take the saying concerning moving a mountain literally. She prayed all night, then on opening her eyes in the morning, she exclaimed, 'I knew all the time it would still be there.' So it is with us. We often pray uncertainly, not discerning the mind of Christ, not knowing whether He will or will not respond, and we do not receive because we ask amiss. Jesus when on earth could at times do no mighty works because of men's unbelief, and He is limited in the same way now by ours.

What then is this 'faith' that He wants? I have defined it elsewhere as 'the acceptance with conviction of an idea *in the presence of spiritually apprehended grounds* for its acceptance',[1] which then issues in the appropriate response as surely as the ideo-reflex due to suggestion. Faith is thus a moral and spiritual attitude. Suggestion is the 'acceptance with conviction of an idea *in the absence of logically adequate grounds* for its acceptance'.[2]

Whatever is so accepted with *conviction* tends to issue in the appropriate thought, action or feeling. This is true whether the suggestion is a good one or a bad one, helpful or harmful. *It is our real conviction that decides the issue,* that is why Christ so emphasises belief and faith either in our approach to Him for ourselves or for others. Without that He cannot work in or through us. So in intercession faith is a vital necessity. Many of our prayers are like that of the

[1] A. G. Ikin, *Religion and Psychotherapy*.
[2] W. McDougall, *Social Psychology*, p. 97.

woman **praying** for the removal of the mountain, while not expecting it to go. We pray earnestly, but the undercurrent of unbelief is effective and our prayer is of no avail. We do not really expect it to succeed. We hope it may, we know some prayers do, but we are not quite sure if ours will, and so we prevent the fulfilment of our prayers by our unbelief. What are we to do about it? How can we make our intercessions effective? We know Christ was able to heal body and soul, we believe He is still able, and that prayer is a means through which sufferer or sinner may be brought within the active range of His love, much as the sick of the palsy was brought to Him by His friends in Palestine. Yet again and again we find ourselves praying as if it were magic and by pressing a button, or turning a prayer wheel with so many names on, God can and will do the rest, and again and again we are disappointed. What are the conditions for effective prayer? We saw at the beginning that communion implied moral unity of purpose and sympathy of outlook. Praying doubtfully implies we are not sure whether our desire is in harmony with God's or not. Hence we cannot be sure it will meet with response. This implies we do not know the mind of God, that we are not sharing the mind of Christ in the matter, and He cannot work through our prayers unless we are.

The magical intercession errs in the opposite direction, it assumes that everything we ask for must be God's will and that He will wave a wand and fulfil it. There is belief but not faith in the sense defined as 'the acceptance with conviction in the presence of spiritually apprehended grounds for acceptance'. Faith is a moral and spiritual attitude of mind, reaching out to the highest. It seeks fellowship with the highest and thus enables us to discern the mind of Christ, Who has the power to fulfil that which He inspires us to seek, that we may share with Him in the love of the Father for all His children, those who know Him and those who do not.

Recently I came across a similar definition of faith to my own. It said, 'Faith is to the spirit what suggestion is to the mind.' When St. James said the prayer of a righteous man availeth much, he did not mean to imply that God had favourites to whom He would listen and respond, while He would ignore the request of sinners. But that the righteous man was so morally in tune with the mind of God that he could discern what God's attitude was and thus become a channel through which God's will could become operative on earth, the will that consistently seeks the best for each and all.

You will remember that in the midst of the crowd, when the woman with the issue of blood touched His garment in faith, Christ stopped at once to see who had touched Him, because 'virtue, power, dynamite' had gone out of Him. This seems to imply that from God's end all is ready, that power is available to meet every human need, but that it does not flow forth mechanically. It is available by faith, which is the *response of a person to a person*, a spiritual act or attitude of trust which enables Him to pour forth vitality to meet the need. Secondly, it shows there is no need to plead with God as if He might not want to help. It implies that His desire to help is continuous, and we may therefore turn to Him as confidently as the woman did, sure that He will meet our needs. But let us remember that we do not always realise our deepest needs. If we come to Him in faith He will meet them, but not *necessarily in the order we think*. Some of our genuine puzzles with regard to petitionary prayer arise because He is leading us to seek the fulfilment of His plans, which are far more important—even for ourselves—than our own.

The description of His treatment of the man sick of the palsy is very illuminating. The longer we meditate upon it the more we learn about Christ and His attitude towards disease, as well as the part we play in enabling Him to deal with the problem of evil, which, as Dr. Temple well says, is a problem worthy of Divine solution. The man's friends had tremendous faith in Christ's power to make him whole, or they would never have gone to such lengths as to take the roof off to let him down at the feet of Christ when they could not get in at the door for the crowds. Jesus saw *their* faith and responded to their appeal. But presumably it was his bodily need that had inspired their sympathy, the deeper need that could evoke his own faith they could not see. So Christ, using their faith as a lever almost, turned to him and lifted the burden of sin that prevented his own belief. After which the man knew he could trust Him when He bid him walk because he had done the apparently impossible spiritually. Jesus had evoked the faith that made healing possible, through the faith of his friends bringing him into touch, so that He could first meet the deeper need.

I think we can learn a great deal about effective intercession from these two illustrations, but it is well worth while to consider all the other healing episodes in that Gospel and meditate upon them in the same way. If in Christ we see God at work on earth, then we realise He is like a great wireless power-station. 'I am come that ye might have life, and have it abundantly.' We can receive power if we are tuned in to the right wave-length, but if we are not tuned in, it has no effect upon us. The crowd around felt nothing when they touched Him, the woman with the issue of blood perceived within herself that she was healed. The wave-length of trust, of faith in His willingness and ability to heal, enabled her to pick up and respond to His own intense vitality, lifting her above the weakness of her own exhausted organism, and to respond to the health-giving vitality inpoured into her. Dynamite, δύναμις, had gone forth.

Then still using the same illustration, let us think of the four friends, who were also 'tuned in' to their sympathy with their friend and faith in Christ as able to meet his need. Again the 'tuning in' is personal, not mechanical. Love, sympathy, faith are meaningless apart from those who love, sympathise and believe. We cannot doubt from Christ's reference to *their* faith, not to that of the sick man, that He was able to act upon the man in such a way as to evoke his faith, through the faith of the friends who were in touch both with Him and with their friend. As soon as the barrier of sin which had prevented direct communion with God had been removed, the man could respond joyfully and directly and his deepest need, far beyond the conscious anticipation of the friends, was met.

Now let us apply that to our intercessions. We can become relay stations through which God can transmit His life-giving power to others in need who have as yet not learned to trust Him directly. The man trusted his friends, the friends trusted Christ, and He in turn responded and won the fellowship and trust of the man himself. But we can only relay that with which we are in sympathy. If envy, hatred, jealousy, anger, annoyance, irritation or rebellion are active in us, we cannot relay the life-giving love of God. We distort and twist everything that comes to us, responding to evil in others and setting up a vicious circle. It is only as we seek to radiate the love of God which knows no limit, that pours itself out on just and unjust alike, until it shall have saved all, that we can rise above the limitations of our own self-centredness and become tuned in so that God can act through us. Our feelings must be like in kind to God's, though not in degree, if our sympathy is to relay the healing and forgiving love of God, if we are to become effectual intercessors. We do not have to strain to develop power, only to open ourselves to become channels for His love. But if this is so, we can only pray effectively for needs that have really touched our hearts enough to inspire us with His own spirit of self-giving love. We must start with needs that stir us to rebel against their lack to strive, to fulfil them. As our fellowship grows through learning how He meets those needs, seeing as the four friends did that sin was worse than disease, the range of our effective intercession increases, until we can at last turn to Him saying, 'You know the needs of the world better than I do, You know where best you can relieve and meet them through me. Here I am, use me.' Whereupon, trusting Him, we find our prayer does achieve, does meet the world's need, in concrete cases as the love of Christ constrains us. We saw that meditation, rightly used, led on to natural 'contemplation', a real gripping of our imagination by the spirit of God. We saw also that this evoked a sense of the way we fall short of the demands of God and our own conscience, inducing penitence and bracing our wills, as well as inspiring our worship. So too petition and intercession, which at first start with our own desires for ourselves or our friends, lead on to clearer understanding of the mind of God, until they too inspire us to seek God's way, not ours, and so prepare the way for the Spirit to work through us for the furtherance of the Kingdom of God on earth.

Effective intercession is the fruit of communion with God in Christ, developed through sacrament and prayer and meditation and contemplation, till in spirit we can leap forth to meet a need, fighting 'not uncertainly as one that beateth the air', but with the assurance of the power to fulfil it.

The Goal of Prayer

Psychology shows us clearly that if we are to become healthy in body and spirit we must have some central ideal large enough to gather all our diversities of gifts into harmonious action. The city divided against itself cannot stand. The state of mind described by St. Paul as the 'body of this death', wherein the good that we would, we do not, and the evil that we would not, that we do, calls aloud for some remedy. The divided self is an impotent self. We have seen that if we are to love God we must learn to know Him, and that unless He were willing to be known, unless He were striving to make Himself known, we should not even know there was a God to know.

Throughout this chapter we have seen that we have been made with minds that are capable of growing into fuller fellowship with the Divine through the use of fundamental laws of human nature, revealed in all men in some degree, but supremely in Christ. We have seen throughout the ages man's impulse to pray. This found its fulfilment in perfect communion in Christ, which led His disciples to ask Him to teach them how to pray. We found the key-note of the pattern prayer was the coming of the Kingdom of Our Father upon earth, and Christ told us that it is the Father's good pleasure to give us the Kingdom. Here then is an ideal that can harness all man's energies. The Kingdom of Heaven *on earth*, and I would emphasise *earth*. We are not meant to be visionaries dreaming of kingdoms in the clouds, of what can be and may be under other conditions. We are here to bring the world in which *we* live into harmony with the laws of the spiritual universe whose beginning and end is love. Heaven is not ready made, even by God. We can only share it as we share in the travail of the ages to bring it into being. And for this everyone counts. There is a little bit for each of us to do that no one else can do, in bringing God's dream of a happy universe true, wherein sin and sorrow have been overcome.

For this we must labour and learn about the conditions under which we live, must work with hand and brain and heart, if the vision of the Kingdom of God, wherein all live in fellowhip, in peace, love and joy, is to be realised on earth. We must learn to see things as they are if we are to help to make them what they ought to be. It is no use having our heads in the clouds which hide the reality of suffering children, depraved lives, starving peoples, and thinking we have risen above the limitations of earth and are therefore members of the Kingdom of Heaven. If we are to bring help to those in distress, we must have our feet firmly planted on the earth.

We must be able to weep with those who weep if we are to rejoice with those who rejoice. The Stoics, scorning suffering, despised the weak. Jesus, who could cry 'I thirst', was moved with compassion. He was not ashamed of human weakness, but entered into it and shared it: and by sharing it thus He alleviated it.

Spirituality and fellowship are synonymous. It is in vital living relationships that true spirituality can develop. The social nature of man unfulfilled by the spiritual is certainly incomplete; though it is the expression of instincts without which he cannot live. But the spiritual that scorns the dust of the earth, that does not embody itself in the flesh and blood of everyday life, ignores the fact that Our Lord Himself was a carpenter, not an angel.

We see nothing truly in heaven unless we first see it on earth. Real persons of prayer are no more produced by fostering a talent than real musicians are by practising scales: though the latter may be necessary for the capacity to be expressed adequately. The man who begins to share the mind of Christ cannot help sharing the mind of his fellows. The man who begins to share in the mind of his fellows is driven back upon the Christ to fulfil their needs. So the solid, unbreakable circle of prayer is begun.

If we would see how the life of the Kingdom of Heaven is to be lived on earth, we must turn to Christ for our example. What do we see? One who spoke as never man spoke before; One who was not ashamed of daily toil, who loved his work, whether as carpenter or teacher; One who lived amidst just the conditions we do, amidst jealousies, misunderstandings, hatreds, fears, prejudices and unbelief, yet who always looked for and found the best in man. One whom little children loved, who was not too pre-occupied with the problems of the world, to take them in His arms and bless them. One who rejoiced in the Father's love and care for all—'their angels do always behold my Father's face'—'the Father Himself loveth you'—

'the very hairs on your head are numbered'. Yet One who could be stern—who was under no illusions as to the motives of those who sought to maintain their own superiority. One who could say, 'Except ye be born again, ye cannot *see* the Kingdom of Heaven', yet could take a little child and say, 'Of such is the Kingdom of Heaven'.

No, Christ had no illusions as to the state of things on earth. He saw the very worst, but it did not blind Him to the possibilities of its becoming the very best. But He never promised a primrose path to the Kingdom of Heaven.

Sin was real, evil had become actual, disease was rampant, hatred, suspicion, distrust, was the opposite of the kingdom of love. So he foresaw that all who followed Him in His splendidly daring refusal to accept the present state of things as of God would meet with opposition from those who must either destroy the challenge to their way of life or change it. But he had no doubt of the final issue. 'It is the Father's good pleasure to give you the kingdom.' The resources are in God. Therefore we can go forward confidently, sure that in the long run love will have overcome evil, and the travail of the ages be fulfilled. But if it is to be so, we may not rest on our oars. We are going to be dead weights carried along by the labours of others, or we may pull just hard enough to counterbalance our own weight and so cease to be a hindrance, or we may put our whole effort into striving to carry the boat a little further up stream.

To any who are willing to live dangerously, to follow Christ in His magnificent refusal to accept evil as final or necessary, He says, 'Let him take up his cross and deny himself and follow me'—and paradoxically, 'Take my yoke upon you, for my yoke is easy and my burden is light.' Only as we go do we find this is true. His way works. The boat does move upstream, somewhat erratically at first, but more and more surely as we settle down to a steady stroke. While with every stroke some fragment of evil is destroyed.

But if we follow Him thus, we find, as He did, that prayer becomes a vital necessity.

Let us look for a moment at this side of His life. He went up into a mountain to pray. Again and again before critical activities, such as the choice of the Apostles, we find Him withdrawing in prayer, that He may share the mind of the Father. Before His passion, on the mount of transfiguration, we learn the Father's response. Moses and Elias talk of His death. He knows what lies ahead. Again in Gethsemane He wrestles in prayer to bring His will into such union with the Father's that He may fulfil the will of Him who sent Him. And every time He comes back with the peace of God within Him that enables Him to act efficiently and intelligently on *earth*.

So, too, we find we cannot keep our poise unless we turn to Him. Evil, distraction, worry, restlessness get on the top of us. Only as we learn, as we have seen, to commune with Him can we abide in Him and let His love become operative on earth. Life is all one, and if we keep our prayer life apart from our daily life, we shall fail. Only as they interpenetrate, so that love for God and love for man blend, can we fulfil the law in love. Some turn to religion to escape the duties of life, others to fulfil them. Whenever our prayer is a real communion it will bring us nearer to man as well as to God, and its test in life is the only test we have. The pattern and standard of life on earth is shown in Christ, who came as man to show us the Father and the Son, one in the spirit of love, which is poured forth on us, that receiving the spirit of adoption we too may cry 'Abba', 'Father', thus once again ending, where we began, with God.

CHAPTER VIII

Further Notes on Prayer

SOME questions may remain in connection with the kind of petitionary and intercessory prayer that is legitimate. We have seen that true prayer is not an attempt to coerce or pester God into doing what *we* want, but an attempt to align ourselves with reality so as to become able to do what He wants and to find our real freedom in His service.

Can we rightly pray for a fine day for *our* garden fête, for example, and if it rains in spite of that, has God failed us, or have we failed to understand the laws of effective prayer?

I think that it is right and healthy to express our desires and hopes freely in our prayers, and that the attempt only to pray for what we think we *ought* to want instead of for what we *do* want brings an element of unreality into and falsifies the relationship with God so that He can neither give us what we want nor what He in His greater wisdom may see to the truer satisfaction of our real needs than our own desires would bring.

If we pray as members of a family, realising that not all our hopes and desires can be fulfilled without frustrating some of the needs of others, we can sincerely ask for what we want if it can be supplied without interfering with God's plans for the whole of the family, and then instead of feeling frustrated if the immediate need is not fulfilled, we find a real gain in the sense of fellowship within the whole that *is* an answer to the prayer.

A personal example may illustrate this. I had put all the money I could raise into getting a hut to turn into a library, and had felt sure this was what God wanted to enable me to work in spite of being physically handicapped. I had prayed for a fine week-end for it to be erected while the man from the works could superintend the local labour I had had to get to help him. Then, when the walls were up and only one night clear was needed to get a roof on, it poured down from 2.30 p.m. to 9 a.m. The walls were sodden and the floor a sea of mud.

As I lay in bed listening to the rain I found myself asking why, since I was sure getting the hut was what God wanted, that should have happened for the *only* night it had no roof on it. It was then that I realised that prayer could never rightly be used to ask for special privileges, even on God's service, and that it was a bigger thing to share in the ups and downs of everyday life and overcome such difficulties as befell others than to expect 'protection' even for special work. My prayer *was* answered, not by the stopping of the rain that was spoiling my new home, whose erection was a real venture of faith, but by participating in a wider fellowship and learning to make the best of what happened and face the prolonged task of drying it out. God *had* provided the shell of the hut which was essential to the work, but all the ordinary difficulties of building, labour, weather conditions had to be overcome. As I lay and listened to that awful drip, drip, drip, I *knew* it was better than 'exemption' and yet that it had also been right to express my very strong desire for the fine week-end for erecting the hut for which I had managed with so much difficulty to get labour, in my prayer. My prayer had been for something I could see my way to, and I was led through it to something I could *not* control or see how to handle, and in trying to face up to it, was led to a deeper understanding of God's ways which enabled me to be *thankful* for the very happening that destroyed my original hope and strong desire.

That is the way in which prayer really *is* answered. The Mind of God *has* brought something fresh into the situation, so that it is not just the 'No' to our original petition, but the discovery of a wider setting within which a 'Yes' would have been a worse answer.

Daniel Poling, in *Faith is Power*, quotes examples of both

'Yes' and 'No' answers to prayer, and shows that in his experience if the answer *is* 'No' then there is also the assurance that under the circumstances that *was* better than the original request.

This sounds like the 'have it both ways' argument that is so irritating to the person who has never really put his faith to the test. But there is a real difference between events that happen 'naturally' and the real self-commitment in prayer connected with some desire for one's self or another. Where this is genuine, then events may have a different issue than if no one had prayed, and when the fundamental attitude is that of seeking God's way for the family, i.e. the Kingdom of God, then if this brings a 'No' to even strong personal wishes, the fulfilment of the bigger issue *is* a gain and faith is strengthened and not weakened by the 'No'.

What of intercession then? Can we rightly pray for healing if we know that 'natural causes' will automatically produce death? I think we can, though the answer will not always involve healing. There are too many cases in recent literature that show the influence of prayer on physical conditions for them all to be dismissed as mistaken diagnoses, hysterical conditions or frankly unbelieved. Psychotherapy, which heals the body through the mind, is showing there is a closer link between physical, mental and spiritual processes than was formerly realised. The development of psychosomatic medicine shows how worry can actually produce stomach ulcers. And if worry can so modify secretions adversely, then faith and hope can influence them for good. It is more reasonable to pray for recovery from illness now than when bodies, minds and spirits were supposed to be separate and only a 'miracle' suspending natural laws could bring about cure.

The harmful results of worry, resentments, anger and greed: the mixture of pride and inferiority in the neurotic, all issue in disorders of physical functioning. The results of peace, faith, hope, love, forbearance, tolerance and understanding must have an opposite effect and increase well-being. Prayer which helps to integrate and unify the conflicting elements of personality is thus an aid to physical health making the most of actual differences in constitution and capacity. It is actually surprising to realise how much of the world's best work is done by those with some real handicaps, who have learned how to triumph through them. The late President Roosevelt is a good example of this.

Another development which makes prayer for others more reasonable than when we were thought to be self-contained and isolated 'individuals' is the work of parapsychologists. Telepathy, clairvoyance and precognition are once again accredited as real and not indications of mental disorder. Though it is not yet possible to see *how* their activities come into play, nor are they under the control of the will, they do bring some of the New Testament stories within the range of actual happenings, today, and not a mythical accretion round the figure of Christ. His perception of the thoughts of Nathaniel while he was making up his mind to approach Christ is an example that leaps to one's mind. The healing of the centurion's servant is also paralleled by the effects of prayer and faith today.

Some people are more open than others to the influence of the moods and feeling of those around them, and if these exert their influence through the 'psi-function', the capacity for extra-sensory perception, then such people would also be more open to healing influences. Some of the differences in response to prayer for healing may well depend on the stage of development of psi-functions. They have been shown not to be strictly proportional to spiritual development or to moral qualities. This is not to rob God of the prerogative of doing more than we can do or can understand. But if we can in some measure remove real intellectual difficulties in the way of believing He can influence the course of events through the extension of human activities in prayer into the spiritual realm that transcends the 'natural' human relationships with each other, it will make it easier to be open to and on the look out for signs of His activity and become responsive to His call.

It is perhaps important to make clear that *effective* prayer does demand that we do anything actually in our power towards the desired result, and don't ask God to do *for* us something He can only do *through* us. To pray as a *substitute* for action is not the prayer that produces results or issues in conviction. When we have done all we can and find our resources are inadequate, then we can rightly pray and help *does* come, though often from unexpected sources which we don't always connect up with our prayers.

We have seen in the Lord's Prayer requests for our needs follow the dedication of our wills to His service. If we pray rightly, then our resources *are* greater than those of people who are self-sufficient and therefore self-limited. But they are *not* resources for personal aggrandisement, prestige or pride of place. They *are* resources for the enriching of human nature, the deepening of friendships, love and facilities for service. And these goods the 'unregenerate' may not desire until the search for selfish happiness has ended in the dust and ashes it must reach. Proofs of answers to prayer which 'ring true' to fellow seekers are not necessarily accepted as proofs by the sceptical and agnostic, since they miss the real significance and try to *explain away* as coincidence the actual effects.

If we have never tried to swim, or have never seen anyone else do so, we would say it was impossible to keep afloat in water, we were so much heavier. And if we start trying with our arms, keeping our feet on the bottom for safety, we can't accept the possibility that the water will bear us up. When we take our feet off and *strike out* we find it does, and the joys of mastering a new element and activity are opened out to us.

So our prayers open a new realm in which in time our first

fumbling efforts issue in skilled action, and increasingly we discover the power of prayer to fulfil and not destroy human freedom and find ourselves members of a wider common-wealth than we had realised. It is then *natural* that things should happen to and through those who pray intelligently, sincerely and regularly that don't happen to those who are closing the door to real spiritual adventure.

To return to prayers for health and healing, some of the most urgent cries that go up to God. What of a mother praying for the life of her sick child, and the child dies? Has God failed to answer? Not necessarily. There was a *specific* cause for that death, and until it is recognised and preventive methods adopted, many will die. But the challenge of a child's death is a stimulus to doctors to research further. The many deaths through diphtheria were not 'wasted' deaths. In time it led to immunising babies and *preventing* instead of merely curing the disease. God's answer did not save the life of the untreated child 'magically' because it was necessary for men to discover how to prevent that kind of disease. And so I think it is with many cases in which prayer does not avert sickness or death. There is something to be learned by either the patient or others through it which could not be learned in any easier way. I don't mean here the development of moral qualities. Some invalids *do* radiate a deep quality of life in spite of their handicaps and sufferings, which is an expression of the fruits of prayer. But the stimulus to research, to discovering *how* the laws of health have been broken, or the nature of some infective agent comes through the failure to cure some sufferers, and these *do* give their lives as part of the great struggle for life on earth. Malaria is a well-known example. The discovery of the mosquito which brings infection leads to the possibility of eliminating the disease by destroying the breeding-grounds of mosquitos.

This, however, does not mean that we should *not* pray for the recovery of someone who has succumbed to disease, or that if we do, recovery should not be expected. The reinforcement of vitality may make the difference between life and death and turn the scales, even in infectious disease. But it is also true that the answer to prayer might be the release from the 'pattern of disease' and the stimulus to others to discover the pattern.

Dr. Rebecca Beard, in *Everyman's Search*, focusses an important *hiatus* in our thinking. A woman doctor herself, she was cured of serious heart trouble through a personal spiritual experience. She felt called to leave the sphere of service medically and to help others to find healing directly. The examples she gives are convincing as to the reality of greater powers of healing and recuperation than are normally met with in hospitals within the environment of prayer and a real faith in Christ's capacity to heal now as He did in Galilee.

The gap she does not fill is that between her former work as a doctor and her later work as spiritual healer or 'metaphysician'. She admits she cannot bridge it. That the two methods seem to be on different planes and are difficult to combine. She has therefore concentrated on the fulfilment of her own spontaneous healing by bringing others into the range of fresh powers.

Her references to psychosomatic medicine *are* a link, but not a complete one. Though it is probable that for the awareness of spiritual reinforcements some such separation is necessary to provide an atmosphere capable of overcoming the mental attitude of the past and some *are* called to lay aside the ordinary remedies and scientific approach to demonstrate the reality of spirit, yet it cannot be right to discard the methods that have brought such an extension of life and the reduction of disease as has come through the medical world. The work Dr. Beard is doing now makes no use of her previous medical training, and could be done by an *equally spiritually mature* lay woman. But it is the *bridge between the two that needs to be built.*

God *does* save lives through the skill of surgeon and physician. He *does* heal mental distress through psychotherapists. He *does* heal through prayer. Many still suffer for lack of the *appropriate* therapy for lack of sufficient skilled and trained men and women to apply even what we do know to meet their need. Yet a greater need is for each type of physician to recognise when the help of the other can go beyond his own skill, as well as the actual stage of development of the patient and the circumstances of his or her life.

Someone once said, 'Some people are on the pill level, some on the mental level and some on the spiritual level', as if it was more spiritual to heal without physical remedies than with them. While it is obviously true that to resort to pills as a substitute for healthy living or facing up to personal problems *is* less spiritual than a real facing up to the demands of life, yet there are remedies so precise, e.g. thyroid for cretinism and insulin for diabetes, that it seems to be presumptuous to expect God to 'intervene' for something we can see how to do, rather like using a sledge hammer to crack a nut. Though on the other hand it is equally important to realise that neuroses are not things that 'happen' to us, but are our ineffective way of reacting to them, and to help a patient to handle his or her own emotional forces better in future so as to outgrow neurotic reactions is a truly *spiritual* process.

Weatherhead, in his recent *Psychology, Religion and Healing*, stressed the importance of discovering the *relevant* way of co-operating with God. He referred to a splinter in someone's eye needing to be taken out by someone, and illnesses of that type, not amenable to prayer as such. It does seem to me that this is more mature than the attempt to specialise on spiritual healing for all types of disease and to leave the medical work behind. We need to know how to draw upon *all* the resources God has provided within the world He has made.

Dr. Beard does recognise people at different stages and does not decry any medical or surgical method for those who still believe in it, and she *has* demonstrated the results of prayer and faith going beyond this. But she does make a complete break with the past and the whole medical attitude herself, and for those who come to her. This is the source of her faith and conviction and would seem to be evidential. But I would like her to try to see how to build her top storey genuinely on the earlier foundations and not make such a complete break. The bridge is one that Dr. Beard should be ideally able to build in the light of her practice on both levels.[1]

It may be difficult to combine the scientific and religious methods and attitudes of mind. But there can be no real 'wholeness' or 'holiness' that does not involve both the material and the spiritual aspects of life. As we saw, man is neither a fallen angel nor a risen ape, but a *unique* being, combining functions shared with the animal world, and a body that functions physiologically like that of other animals with a capacity for recognising meaning and significance, beauty, truth and love for others that distinguishes him from other animals.

His health in the deepest sense must depend upon his ability to combine the two and to add his quota to the wonders of creation by being the best example of the human being it is in him to be.

The separation of the 'wholeness' of the primitive witch-doctor or medicine-man, before his function became differentiated into physician, priest and magician (a differentiation that occurred as early as the sixteenth century B.C.) who combined the religious outlook of his tribe and day with whatever knowledge was available, into the respectable doctor concerned with our bodies and the equally respectable priest concerned with our souls, has led to an inadequate conception of both souls and bodies. This divergence has led to a

[1] Since this was written Dr. Beard has died.

separation of the functional unity of mental and physical processes, and to an ignoring of the actual psychosomatic unity which is so close that we do not yet know whether to speak of body-minds or mind-bodies.

This in turn has led to the development of modern medical psychology in an attempt once more to treat the *whole* human being, with this physiological processes and his hopes, aspirations, fears and sins on the one hand, and to the revival of interest in the ministry of healing on the part of clergy and others, who are beginning to realise that religion must concern itself with the whole man, and not just with his spiritual aspirations or sinfulness.

There is no hard and fast line. Under some conditions, healing processes can be brought into play via mental and spiritual activities that influence physiological functions and health may be restored. While some mental disorders can be relieved by physical means.

Disease is a consequence of disorder on so many levels; poverty, malnutrition, broken homes, accidents, infections all play a part, as well as our attitude to life. No one approach, therefore, can be adequate. All that makes for healthy, wholesome living helps to raise the level for the world. Faith and prayer, therefore, *are* relevant to health—physical health, not just spiritual growth—without ignoring all the other conditions which are necessary. A quiet confident mind can make the best of actual physical resources and give nature a chance to heal some injury or infection, when an over-anxious one may add to the strains on the body. Moreover, we can all help or hinder others through our own attitude. A doctor recently said he had found a patient unexpectedly worse and discovered a neighbour had been in telling her of a friend who had died with similar symptoms, and her anxiety had made her worse, though previously the symptoms had been yielding to treatment. Another doctor had been surprised to find a patient improving more rapidly than he had expected. Then he found this had followed on having had Communion the day before. His comment was, 'Well, if Communion has that effect on you, I don't mind your having it every day.' The patient's reply was illuminating. She said, 'it wouldn't have that effect if I had it for that.' It was only because it was real, for its own sake, that it had incidentally improved the physical condition. (The patient was seriously ill, too weak to feed herself at the time, and the doctor had been afraid the service for which she had asked would be too much for her and was agreeably surprised that it had actually made a considerable difference for the better.)

That attitude sums up this whole question of prayer. The real aim is to grow into fuller and richer communion with God, to reach out beyond our petty egoistic selves into the wider reaches of the Spirit. In and through that communion the forces of spirit find a point of contact with our everyday life which can help and heal pain-racked bodies and sin-distorted minds. If we honestly seek first the Kingdom of God, results follow, though not always the ones we expect. But if we fall back even on God as a 'magic helper', though the intensity of our appeals may produce effects, they will not be lastingly beneficial, and they will be spiritually dangerous. God is able to help us to become more mature, to share more fully in the Mind of Christ through His indwelling spirit. In proportion as we enter into our heritage as 'Sons' we find the resources of His Kingdom are available for the discerning and following of His way for us, and in that service we find our true freedom, and even death is no longer master of life, but becomes its servant, a gateway into a fuller life when our journey here is over and our work on earth done.